T0329014

HOW TO FIND OUT

HOW TO FIND OUT

by

LIONEL McCOLVIN

LONDON
PUBLISHED FOR
THE NATIONAL BOOK LEAGUE
BY CAMBRIDGE UNIVERSITY PRESS
1947

CAMBRIDGE
UNIVERSITY PRESS

University Printing House, Cambridge CB2 8BS, United Kingdom

Cambridge University Press is part of the University of Cambridge.

It furthers the University's mission by disseminating knowledge in the pursuit of
education, learning and research at the highest international levels of excellence.

www.cambridge.org
Information on this title: www.cambridge.org/9781316612026

© Cambridge University Press 1947

First published 1933
Second edition 1947
First paperback edition 2016

A catalogue record for this publication is available from the British Library

ISBN 978-1-316-61202-6 Paperback

CONTENTS

PREFACE TO THE SECOND EDITION

THIS book – and its companion volume *How to Use Books* – was first published in 1933. In this edition the information has been brought up to date, changes in practice during the last twelve years and particulars of new publications and new editions being incorporated. The plan and scope of the book remains unchanged, however. It was and is intended as a brief guide to outstanding and typical sources of information with simple hints on how to discover and exploit them. It was and is deliberately brief because it is written for beginners in the limitless and ever fascinating pursuit of information. Too much detail, at this stage, would have been confusing, but if the book opens only a few doors leading into the wide world of fact it does show the purposive reader a great many more that he can enter if he will.

CHAPTER ONE

KNOWLEDGE AND INFORMATION

WE all like to think that as we grow up, from childhood through youth to manhood and womanhood, we gradually become wiser and better as well as just bigger.

Probably on the whole we do. We learn how to behave without being a nuisance to others; we acquire sympathy and a measure of tolerance; we become better able to adjust ourselves to circumstances, to endure disappointments and to seize opportunities; we accumulate a certain amount of knowledge.

Nevertheless, there are two good habits, practised even to excess in childhood, which many of us gradually lose as we grow older. They are the kindred qualities of curiosity and observation.

In the normal child they are keenly active. He sees and hears and notices everything – including much that his elders think he shouldn't. He misses nothing. He is perpetually seeking to discover the how, why and wherefore of things; ceaselessly asking questions. His curiosity only flags when he realizes, as is often the case, that his parents and teachers are as ignorant as he where such fundamental issues are concerned.

The child *needs* to be curious and observant. If he were not, he would never develop mentally. In this way only can he acquire the knowledge necessary for the business and the pleasure of life.

In time he has gained the necessary minimum. He has sufficient understanding, sufficient knowledge to take a place in the 'grown-up' world; without any conscious effort to know more, content with picking up by the way sufficient new facts and ideas to make up for others he forgets or wears out, he can even manage, after a fashion, to perform some routine work and pass his leisure in stereotyped amusements. But he must merely stagnate. He cannot hope to be a success; if he is not unhappy, it will be simply because he hasn't enough imagination to see what he is missing.

Thousands of men and women – even some who were bright youngsters – do slip all too easily into this unsatisfactory condition. They let those two qualities, which, above all, can make life interesting and valuable, fall into disuse. One is prepared to realize that men are not gifted with equal capabilities, that some men, because of inborn limitations, will never be leaders; but even these can, in their own sphere of life, be valuable, happy mortals if they do not lose their interest in life. For that is what the decay of curiosity really amounts to.

On the other hand, however, quite as many not only retain the faculty for inquiry; they find that, as they grow older, the need for knowledge and information does not diminish but increases. Their life becomes more complex; they are daily brought into contact with new and different circumstances; they are themselves in active competition with others who are no less observant, no less curious, no less determined to know all that need be known. *These* people form the active, progressive, successful, happy section of the community. They realize that they *live* only because they take heed of all the factors that influence them, of all their circumstances and changing conditions, because they realize that the development of personality depends upon the richness of their experience.

From cradle to grave their life is, therefore, a steady, unceasing process of finding out, of increasing understanding, acquiring knowledge, utilizing information.

It may have been noticed that we have spoken of 'knowledge' and 'information' as though they were two different matters. In a sense they are.

On the one hand, we have need for a background, a store of fundamental ideas and essential facts without which we cannot proceed. There are certain things that every intelligent person must *know*; certain foundation ideas which all must accept, since they are the basis of human civilization. These we acquire partly by education, partly from contact with our fellow-men. Furthermore, each one of us must have some grasp of the essential facts involved in our particular type of work and our other occupations. These form our personal equipment; they are the result of study and experience. The greater their extent the better we are fitted for life.

Nevertheless, no matter how good our education, general and vocational, may have been, no matter how good our memories, how keen our intelligence, how comprehensive our knowledge, we can only *know* a very small percentage of existing facts.

And since we are in a world that is constantly changing, since new ideas are continually being formulated and new facts discovered, since none of us can foresee precisely what facts we shall need to meet the situations and solve the problems that will confront us to-morrow, next week, next year, it must be clear that every day we must supplement our knowledge, adding to it the necessary extra data.

Remember that our capacity is limited. We can only take in and retain *so* much; we cannot overburden ourselves with a mass of material just in case we *might* need it. It has been said of Bacon that he knew all that was then to be known. He didn't, of course; whole civilizations existed in other parts of the world of which he knew nothing whatever. But even if we interpret the saying as meaning that Bacon knew all that the science and learning of his time and place could teach him, it must be acknowledged that his was an exceptional intellect and, further, that the body of existing knowledge has increased a hundredfold, at least, since then. To-day it is impossible for the cleverest man to know a thousandth part, not even a millionth, of what there is to be known. Yet it does not by any means follow that any one of us might not have occasion to learn *any* one of the billions of existing facts.

Therefore we must, willy-nilly, divide facts and ideas into two varieties – those we should *know*, and those we must, if need be, *find out*. For convenience' sake the latter may be called 'information'.

It is not, however, easy for those without any experience and guidance to 'find out' all the facts they require. The field of information is an immense one. Nevertheless, though many facts are difficult to find, if not totally inaccessible, a large part of the ground has been thoroughly surveyed and mapped out for the convenience of inquirers. The reader needs to be brought into touch with this readily accessible information and shown how to set about utilizing it. Then not only will he be better equipped for his work, he will, by saving time on the many fairly simple inquiries, have more to devote to the difficult ones.

A famous business man once, when complimented upon his remarkable grasp of detail and up-to-date methods, replied that nevertheless he was by no means a 'well-informed' man; it was not what he *knew* that mattered, but what he could *find out*. So it is with all of us. If we can find out quickly and accurately, the whole realm of learning, science, discovery and history is at our command.

All who have come into touch with the general inquiring public must be struck by the lack of any systematic instruction in this vital matter. Surely it is no less important that young people should be taught how to find out than that they should be given a general basic education. Information is the necessary complement to knowledge. The lad (or the girl) who is taught the few things it is possible to teach him during his brief educational period, but who is *not* taught how to discover the additional information he is bound to require as he goes through life, is sent out into the world only half equipped.

One would think that, considering the value of information, all children would receive instruction in the chief sources and methods – that 'research' would be elevated to a position only a little below the 'three R's', reading, writing and arithmetic. Such, however, is not the case, and though it is to be believed that educationists will soon pay more heed to the subject, at present the general inquirer is greatly in need of guidance.

This little book, therefore, should have a definite value to thousands of men and women in all walks of life who have found themselves thus handicapped. At best it can only be an introduction, but the author believes that even within its necessary limitations it should prove useful. For one thing, though each of us has his own special queries and problems, many of them are of a fairly general character; for another, the methodology of research is the same, whatever the required data may be; thirdly, by presenting typical instances of sources, this book will induce each reader, though his own particular needs may not be covered, to appreciate the nature and extent of the help he may expect to find in his own subject.

The author has spent several years in the reference departments of public libraries, engaged in helping readers of all types, from the working man to the research specialist, to find out a multitude of varied items of information. In that work he has, inevitably, learned something about sources and methods; he has appreciated, also, the difficulties confronting the inexperienced inquirer.

The very wealth of material is bewildering. There are so many possible sources which may or may not be fruitful that the beginner does not know where to begin. He cannot look everywhere; he may waste considerable time looking in the least likely places, when the expert would turn naturally to the *most* likely.

He does not realize that a vast amount of information has been assembled systematically for the benefit of inquirers. Though for *some* facts long search is necessary, quite a majority are ready to hand. Experience has shown that a few dozen outstanding reference books, indeed, include more than half the facts that a succession of average inquirers are seeking; if you know these books, perhaps a majority of your queries can be answered in a few minutes, but, more important, if you do *not* know them and look further afield your task may be immense. This is because the compilers of these storehouses of knowledge naturally concentrated on data which, until then, was *not* easily discovered.

Thirdly, the beginner is apt to become disheartened. He is too ready, after a brief unsuccessful search, to come to the conclusion that the needed information is not available. The expert knows that there are very few things he *cannot* find out if he devotes sufficient time to the inquiry.

Time, nevertheless, is a vital factor. How much trouble it is worth your while to devote to any inquiry will depend upon the value of the information when found. There is always a limit, however, beyond which it would be unprofitable to go. In every instance, speed is important. And speed can only come with experience and knowledge of likely sources. Much information is wanted urgently, immediately the need arises.

Information is to be found in many places, the chief of which are mentioned in the following pages. The main division is that between published and unpublished information. The former is found in books, newspapers, periodicals, maps and other printed matter; the latter is preserved in the private records of men and organizations, perhaps existing only in their memories.

For convenience the author deals first with books of all kinds, because these are the most accessible of all sources of information – especially to-day when everyone can make free use of public and other libraries. As the scope and resources of these invaluable institutions were discussed in the companion volume *How to Use Books*, this information is not repeated in this book. It is assumed throughout that readers make full use of library facilities, that they are 'book-users'.

Next we consider periodicals and a number of other types of published records with which the inquirer should be acquainted.

As a general principle, turn first to published sources. They embrace most of the existing facts; they are the handiest and quickest sources. Nevertheless, when they fail to produce results the search need not come to an end. Though much information has not been recorded and published for public use, it is known to individual experts or to organizations which often exist for the collection and utilization of knowledge. As a rule you will find these willing to help you unless, of course, the facts you require are not available to the general public. Some information is 'private', either because it would not be to the interest of the community to make it public or because those who possess it have spent time and money in acquiring it for their own personal benefit. Otherwise, when you have exhausted the published sources, you can turn to the unpublished ones.

Throughout, the author's aim is to give as much guidance as possible, to draw attention to the maximum number of useful sources. The result may not be a very readable book, but if the reader will regard it rather as a textbook, as a compendium, and devote a little while to its various suggestions, it is hoped that the time saved in future inquiries will compensate for present study.

The author would, indeed, have been happy if the theme and the available space had permitted a more interesting treatment, for then it might have served to induce many who have not done so already to develop their faculty for inquiry. Perhaps it may do so in spite of its shortcomings. No book could serve a better purpose.

The inquiring mind is the happy, the active mind. We grow old, mentally, as soon as and not until we cease to be interested in the world around us and the people we meet.

We have noted the practical value of inquiry in connection with work and studies. We have seen the need for discovering facts and more facts. Nevertheless, taking all things into consideration, the writer is not sure that curiosity for curiosity's sake, inquiry for inquiry's sake, is not just as important. It is the inquiring spirit that keeps the mind healthy. If our work doesn't provide sufficient physical exercise to keep our bodies healthy, we engage in sports; similarly, if our work does not provide ample mental exercise, we must find it by developing our curiosity.

And so, although the following pages may give the impression that they are intended only for the earnest student, they are equally a guide to the less serious mortal who has no material motive but to keep his mind alert.

You may have obvious needs for information. If you haven't, create them. Whatever you do, start asking questions. It is astonishing how much more interesting the simplest occupation, the most ordinary activity, can become if you start asking questions about it. And the surprising thing is that once you start inquiring for inquiry's sake you will find that these questionings, at first aimless and purposeless, gradually assume practical value and importance. They somehow lead to useful activity.

Do not think that for inquiry to give pleasure it need be complicated. The simplest fact, tracked down because it is of interest, is as keen a stimulus, as valuable a mental tonic. All that matters is that you should want to use your mind and exercise your curiosity.

CHAPTER TWO

GENERAL REFERENCE BOOKS

THE inquirer will, at times, have to make use of many different kinds of books, often quite 'unlikely' ones. Nevertheless, he will usually turn first to books which have been designed especially for those who want to 'find out' something, books which are not written to be 'read' or studied, but which are storehouses of data so arranged that each fact can be found with the minimum of trouble.

These are called 'reference books' – those to which we 'refer', to which we bring our questions just as we might ask friends and teachers for information.

There are several types of reference books, some covering a wide field, others concerned with special provinces of knowledge. Some of them are so important and comprehensive that everyone should be acquainted with their scope and arrangement. Their use should be taught in school, for surely every few days, perhaps every few hours, occasion must arise when each one of us might, with advantage, turn to an encyclopaedia, a dictionary, WHITAKER'S ALMANACK, or some similar work of universal interest. Yet, strange though it may seem, there are probably hundreds of thousands of intelligent people who neglect their aid, who do not even know that such books exist.

Foremost among reference books are the two closely related types, *encyclopaedias and dictionaries*, of which succeeding examples have served students for many centuries.

The encyclopaedia is the older form and is named after the Greek words meaning 'complete education'. The first encyclopaedias, though they were not so called, dealt with all those studies which the Greek youth had to complete before he was considered properly prepared for life. They were, therefore, really comprehensive textbooks. The first known example was compiled by a disciple of Plato more than three hundred years before Christ, but the most notable classical work was the NATURAL HISTORY of Pliny the Elder (A.D. 77). Covering a much wider field than we should now understand by the title, and dealing not only with all branches of science, but also with such matters as geography, medicine, and the history of the arts, it embraced nearly forty thousand facts, which were drawn from two thousand books by at least one hundred different authors. Its compiler's industry was, however, rewarded – if service to one's fellow-men is sufficient recompense – for it remained in use throughout the dark ages. Some idea of its popularity is indicated by the fact that between the time when printing was invented and 1536, a hundred years, no fewer than forty-three different editions were printed. There are not many books that can live for fifteen centuries. Several similar comprehensive 'popular educators' – though probably the students of the Middle Ages would not approve of the adjective – appeared throughout the succeeding centuries and in many countries. Surely the most *remarkable* of all encyclopaedias, however, was that prepared at the beginning of the eighteenth century for the Chinese Emperor, K'ang hi, and running to five thousand and twenty volumes! A copy in the British Museum is bound up into seven hundred volumes.

These early encyclopaedias were, as already stated, comprehensive collections of information intended for study. Later, however – perhaps because students began to realize the hopelessness of trying to *learn* so much – they became works of reference. In the meantime dictionaries, though not of the type we use now, were being compiled, and it was inevitable that sooner or later someone would have the idea of arranging all the knowledge in an encyclopaedia in alphabetical order, since, if this could be achieved, no handier method could exist.

The first dictionaries were, as before said, not the com-

prehensive lists of practically all the words in the language
which we now expect them to be. The earliest known dictionary was a lexicon to the works of Homer. In the second
century after Christ one of the earliest Greek dictionaries
was compiled, but the words were arranged not in alphabetical order, but according to meaning. The most notable
Greek dictionary, that of Suidas, was more a collection of
odds and ends of biography and history, with extracts from
various writers, than a 'word-book', while the earliest
English dictionary – if the term may be applied to such a
book – was an attempt to explain, in Latin, the meaning of
English words, the PROMPTORIUM PARVULORUM compiled by
a Dominican monk in 1440.

However, to return to encyclopaedias: though he was not
the first to think of using alphabetical order, a Franciscan
friar, Vincenzo Coronelli, must be given the credit of being
the first to attempt to prepare an alphabetical encyclopaedia
on a large scale. It was only an attempt, for though he
proposed to explain some three hundred thousand words
in a series of forty-five large volumes, of which the first
appeared in 1701, he only finished seven, and they were,
alas, very hurried and inaccurate. But it was a brave
attempt.

Working on less ambitious lines, John Harris (1667-1719),
a London clergyman, published, in 1708-10, the first English
alphabetical encyclopaedia. The two volumes were devoted
to the arts and sciences, and embraced a number of admirable mathematical and astronomical tables.

Much more important, however, since it was the fore-
runner of the modern encyclopaedia, was that of Ephraim
Chambers, whose two volumes (1728) were translated into
French, and provided a model for the great French encyclopaedia of Diderot and D'Alembert, a work which achieved
distinction as much because its authors used it as a medium
for revolutionary propaganda as to promote learning.
Ephraim Chambers improved upon his predecessors by in-
venting a system of references. Under each article he

referred to the wider subject to which it belonged and also to the various parts of which mention was made under more definite headings. As this leads us directly to one of the main difficulties confronting encyclopaedists, be they eighteenth century or modern, this is an appropriate point at which to leave this historical introduction and turn to the survey of current encyclopaedias.

From the foregoing it will be seen that *all* of them are not arranged alphabetically, though most are—the dictionary definition of the word is 'a book giving information on all branches of knowledge or of one subject, usually arranged alphabetically; a general course of instruction'; the essential element of an encyclopaedia is its comprehensive character. Note also that the word 'dictionary' is often used as a synonym for 'encyclopaedia'. For instance, GROVE'S DICTIONARY OF MUSIC and THORPE'S DICTIONARY OF APPLIED CHEMISTRY are, in the generally accepted use of the word, encyclopaedias, many of the entries being lengthy articles.

In the *alphabetical encyclopaedia* we find a series of descriptions and explanations of all the matters embraced by the book (in the case of a 'general' encyclopaedia this means *all* matters of general interest), arranged in one alphabetical order of the names of the subjects described. Thus it is very easy, as a rule, to find what we need. The chief difficulties are, firstly, that we may not think of the particular word under which our subject will be arranged, and secondly that subjects are closely associated and part of the information may be under one heading and part under another.

The first of these difficulties is surmounted by the use of cross references. If we look under the wrong heading we are told to turn to whichever word is used, though with the best system of cross references you will need often to think of as many likely headings as you can. There are always a few possible entry words, only one of which can be chosen.

For example:

> Wales, New South (*see* New South Wales).
> Walhalla (*see* Valhalla).
> Wallaby (*see* Kangaroo).
> Walking (*see* Athletics).

The second difficulty is treated by references, at the end of each article, to other related headings. Never fail to make use of them if the first article does not answer the question.

For example, at the end of the article on the 'War Office' (in the EVERYMAN'S ENCYCLOPÆDIA) we are told to '*see* Staff, Army. *See further* under Army – Army Organization'.

Most encyclopaedias give the information under the most specific heading possible – that is to say, under the name of the smallest subject, the separate individual matter, and not under the larger theme of which it may be a part.

The largest and most important encyclopaedia, however, does not completely adopt this method throughout. This,

THE ENCYCLOPÆDIA BRITANNICA, 14TH EDITION, 24 vols., 1929 (new edition in preparation),

instead provides much longer and more thorough articles on important subjects and branches of knowledge – as well as numerous specific entries – and, in order that the needed facts might not be lost to the inquirer because they appear under a heading to which he might not turn, there is a very full index to the whole work. This index *must* be used frequently.

The first edition of this famous work, undoubtedly the best of its kind, appeared as long ago as 1768, when it consisted of only three volumes, first issued in sixpenny parts. It is now the fundamental reference book, the one to which, in most cases, unless the data you require is more recent or specialized, you will turn *first*. It is very comprehensive, and the ordinary reader may not have sufficient use for it to justify purchasing it for his own use, but he will certainly find it in every library of any pretensions.

The articles are by authorities, the illustrations are

plentiful and good and, so far as is possible in *any* twenty-four volumes, it covers the whole field of knowledge. As before said, the tendency is to include long articles which are really brief introductions to the subjects, compressed but readable, and thus valuable to the student; but by availing yourself of the index you will find it no less useful for general reference purposes because of that.

The last completely revised edition of the ENCYCLOPÆDIA BRITANNICA, the 14th, appeared in 1929, but a certain amount of 'continuous revision' has been incorporated in later printings. Moreover, in 1938 there appeared the first

ENCYCLOPÆDIA BRITANNICA BOOK OF THE YEAR,

embracing articles on more recent events and much revision of older material.

The ENCYCLOPÆDIA BRITANNICA is now an Anglo-American publication, though it tends to pay rather more attention to British than to American interests and outlook. The reverse is true of its principal competitor –

THE ENCYCLOPÆDIA AMERICANA

or just AMERICANA as later editions are styled. It also is a 'continuously revised' encyclopaedia, in 30 vols., and also has a yearly supplement,

THE AMERICANA ANNUAL.

Two smaller British encyclopaedias must now be mentioned –

EVERYMAN'S ENCYCLOPÆDIA, 12 vols., 1931-32,

and

CHAMBERS'S ENCYCLOPÆDIA, 10 vols., 1923-27.

Both are on the short article, 'specific topic', plan. Moreover, apart from being much less expensive and easier to house and to handle, they do in fact contain information not to be found in the larger works. This is inevitable because the field of knowledge is so immense that the editors of even the largest encyclopaedias can present only a small part and the selection of different editors is bound to vary. This remark may seem a glimpse of the obvious but we would remind our fact-finder that it applies to all kinds of reference books. It is thus most unwise to overlook the smaller and cheaper works. We have often found the facts we sought in a sixpenny book when a six guinea book had failed us – though, obviously, the bigger and better the book the greater the likelihood of satisfaction.

We are happy to announce that completely new editions of both EVERYMAN'S ENCYCLOPÆDIA and CHAMBERS'S ENCY-CLOPÆDIA are in course of preparation – the latter to be published now by Geo. Newnes, Ltd.

Incidentally we would mention that

HUTCHINSON'S PICTORIAL ENCYCLOPAEDIA

is practically the same as EVERYMAN'S ENCYCLOPÆDIA, with a great many more illustrations and the text substantially reduced, some articles being omitted and others shortened.

There should be a good encyclopaedia in every household. It will quickly repay its cost many times over, settling those innumerable questions of fact which arise in conversation and in one's reading, helping the children with their studies and affording an inexhaustible mine to be 'dipped into' at odd moments. Incidentally, a man who has an encyclopaedia, WHITAKER'S ALMANACK, or even a timetable with which to amuse himself need never fear boredom.

EVERYMAN'S and CHAMBERS'S are both ideal encyclopaedias for the home library, but for those who cannot obtain or afford them there are several one-volume encyclopaedias to be recommended.

The largest of these:

THE COLUMBIA ENCYCLOPEDIA, 1935,

(published in England by Harrap) is such a large volume that it must contain about half as many words as either of the two works just mentioned.

Much smaller, handy octavo volumes are:

ODHAM'S GREAT ENCYCLOPEDIA OF UNIVERSAL KNOW-
LEDGE

and

ROUTLEDGE'S UNIVERSAL ENCYCLOPAEDIA,

both published not long before the war, and packed full of concise data.

When using encyclopaedias remember that there are various alternative methods of alphabetical arrangement. For example, when the heading consists of two or more words the arrangement can be either by the first word with further arrangement according to the second, e.g.

        War.

        War Compensation Court.

        War debts.

        War graves.

        War medals, etc.,

or the two words can, for alphabeting purposes, be considered as one long one, in which case the entries starting with war will be separated by other words, in this manner:

        War.

        Warbeck.

        Warburton.

        War Compensation Court.

        Ward.

        War debts.

        Warden.

        Wardroom.

        Wareham.

        War graves, etc.

This may seem a trivial point, but in a large encyclopaedia the second method (adopted by both the BRITANNICA and EVERYMAN) may separate articles by dozens of pages. In this particular instance, in the BRITANNICA, 'War Trade Department' appears fifty pages after 'War'. Clearly, the careless inquirer, ignorant of the method adopted, can easily miss the required article.

Very much akin to the encyclopaedia is the *dictionary*, particularly what is known as the *encyclopaedic dictionary* which, in addition to an account of the meaning, derivation and pronunciation of the words, gives a brief description and, perhaps, an illustration.

The best 'encyclopaedic dictionaries' are all American.

THE CENTURY DICTIONARY AND CYCLOPÆDIA, 12 vols., 1911,

is a very fine production, rich in technical terms, and with full descriptive material and thousands of illustrations. The last volume is an atlas, while the eleventh (which may be obtained separately) is

THE CENTURY CYCLOPÆDIA OF NAMES.

This is a particularly important book, because nothing quite like it exists, and you will have innumerable occasions to use it. It embraces names in geography, biography, mythology, history, ethnology, art, architecture, fiction, etc., and gives their pronunciation. There are several useful appendices, including chronological and genealogical tables.

THE NEW CENTURY DICTIONARY, 3 vols., 1927,

is a shorter version incorporating some new material.

THE NEW STANDARD DICTIONARY, PUBLISHED BY FUNK AND WAGNALL, 2 vols., 1913,

is similar in type but shorter. There is also a smaller, one-volume edition.

Another admirable American work is

WEBSTER'S NEW INTERNATIONAL DICTIONARY, 1939.

'Webster' has almost become a synonym for 'dictionary', and not without reason, for it is well edited and reliable, and the definitions are notably clear. It is in one volume, but *what* a volume. Weighing several pounds, it is far too heavy to handle with ease. There are, however, various smaller versions of Webster, such as WEBSTER'S COLLEGIATE DICTIONARY.

For convenience' sake we need – in the home and the office – one or other of the smaller 'desk' dictionaries, keeping the larger ones for reference when these fail.

Here the best are English publications:

THE CONCISE OXFORD DICTIONARY, 1929,

a small volume, though it contains 1460 pages, based upon the monumental NEW ENGLISH DICTIONARY (see later), and

CHAMBERS'S TWENTIETH CENTURY DICTIONARY, 1927,

are recommended, though there are others equally good such as CASSELL'S NEW ENGLISH DICTIONARY, NUTTALL'S STANDARD DICTIONARY and EVERYMAN'S ENGLISH DICTIONARY (published by Dent in 1942). Examine and compare them at your bookseller's.

The most recent larger English dictionary, published in June 1932, is

THE UNIVERSAL DICTIONARY OF THE ENGLISH LANGUAGE, EDITED BY H. C. WYLD.

It is in one large quarto volume and embraces some 200,000 words. Special attention is paid to the history of words and changes in their meaning, and there are copious illustrative phrases. The pronunciation of every word is indicated in two ways: by a simple method that can be readily understood by anyone who has a knowledge of English, and by a more exact system of phonetic notation for students and foreign users. There is a good list of abbreviations at the end.

The great dictionary, however, is

THE NEW ENGLISH DICTIONARY ON HISTORICAL PRINCIPLES, 10 vols., 1888-1928.

Often referred to as 'Murray's' dictionary (as Sir James Murray was its principal editor) and as the 'Oxford' dictionary (as it is published by the Oxford University Press), this marvellous work was compiled on a plan different from that of all other dictionaries. Designed to show the history of words, when they were first used and the changes they have undergone, a valuable feature is the series of quotations illustrating the development of the English language. It includes 414,825 words, and 1,827,306 quotations, including thousands of words no longer in use. A SUPPLEMENT of new words and words previously omitted was published in 1933. See also

THE SHORTER OXFORD ENGLISH DICTIONARY, 2 vols., 1936.

The best *'etymological' dictionaries* – in which particular attention is paid to the derivation of words – are

SKEAT'S ETYMOLOGICAL DICTIONARY OF THE ENGLISH
LANGUAGE,

and

WEEKLEY'S ETYMOLOGICAL DICTIONARY OF MODERN
ENGLISH,

the latter being the more up to date.

Most dictionaries have, usually at the beginning, a few
pages telling how the dictionary is arranged, how to use it,
what abbreviations have been adopted, how pronunciation
is indicated, etc. You will save hours later on and avoid
misunderstandings if you make a proper study of these
pages. If you were a carpenter you would, before you
started work, learn how to use your tools; reference books
are tools – learn how to handle *them*.

The user of words – the reader and especially the writer –
may want still further help which the ordinary dictionary
cannot give. For example, even experts will argue whether
certain phrases, spellings and word combinations are 'correct'. To mention but a few such disputed points – is it
correct to say 'different to'? Is it better to ask your butcher
for 'sirloin' or 'surloin'? Do you know that 'A goodly apple
rotten at the core' and 'A poor thing but mine own' are
both misquotations, none the less wrong because they are
always misquoted? Guidance regarding these and thousands
of other difficulties is to be found in

H. W. FOWLER'S DICTIONARY OF MODERN ENGLISH
USAGE, 1929.

Those who read American novels and see American
films – and who doesn't? – will find

H. W. HORWILL'S DICTIONARY OF MODERN AMERICAN
USAGE, 1935

very useful as it compares and contrasts words which have
different meanings and different forms in English and
American.

Then there are *dictionaries of synonyms* – words which
have the same or similar meanings – and antonyms –
words which mean the opposite to one another. All who

have occasion to write know how desirable it is to select the exact word that will express their meaning, how often the wise use of synonyms will prevent clumsy repetitions; moreover, by using these dictionaries, it is easy to increase one's vocabulary. When, in lighter moments, we try to solve crossword puzzles they are invaluable.

The earliest, and still one of the best, is

GEORGE CRABB'S ENGLISH SYNONYMS EXPLAINED.

First published in 1816, there have been many editions. All the words and phrases are carefully distinguished – a vital point, as hardly any words have *exactly* the same meaning.

Other good dictionaries of *synonyms* are those of E. B. ORDWAY, C. J. SMITH, J. C. FERNALD and R. SOULE, but the most famous work of this kind is

ROGET'S THESAURUS OF WORDS AND PHRASES.

This is not a dictionary – though a very full index serves as one – for the words and expressions are fully classified, with the antonyms in parallel columns. At first sight it seems very complicated, but this difficulty is more apparent than real. Somewhat akin are

F. J. WILSTACK'S DICTIONARY OF SIMILES,

and

MARCH'S THESAURUS DICTIONARY OF THE ENGLISH LANGUAGE.

The poet is provided with *rhyming dictionaries.* Superior persons may smile at them, but if they did not serve some useful purpose the well-known examples would certainly not have retained their popularity for so long. WALKER'S is the most famous; LORING'S RHYMER'S LEXICON and WALTER RIPMAN'S POCKET DICTIONARY OF ENGLISH RHYMES are also recommended.

Next, as several thousands of *abbreviations and contractions* of all kinds are in frequent everyday use, we need some guide to their meaning. Shorter lists are usually included in general dictionaries and encyclopaedias; there is a brief one in WHITAKER'S ALMANACK and another, mostly

confined to degrees, orders, decorations, etc., in WHO'S WHO.
See also

F. H. COLLINS' AUTHORS' AND PRINTERS' DICTIONARY,
'a guide for authors, editors, printers, correctors of the
press, compositors and typists', which, though primarily
concerned with 'usage', spelling, etc., includes a list of
abbreviations.

The most complete works, however, are

H. J. STEPHENSON'S 'ABBREV'
– an American publication –

ERIC PARTRIDGE'S DICTIONARY OF ABBREVIATIONS
and

W. T. ROGERS' DICTIONARY OF ABBREVIATIONS OF TERMS
USED IN PROFESSIONS, SPORTS, TRADES AND LAW.

As you will discover by reference to MINTO'S REFER-
ENCE BOOKS, MADGE'S GUIDE TO REFERENCE BOOKS and
MCCOLVIN'S LIBRARY STOCK, there are also various dictionaries
of obsolete words, Americanisms, provincialisms, dialects and
slang. The last are not, of course, primarily intended to
enable you to extend your vocabulary but whether this is
your purpose – and an 'extensive vocabulary' may on occasion
be useful – or whether you merely seek enlightenment,
consult

ERIC PARTRIDGE'S DICTIONARY OF SLANG AND UNCON-
VENTIONAL ENGLISH
and

L. V. BERRY and M. VAN DEN BARK'S AMERICAN
THESAURUS OF SLANG.

So much for English dictionaries.

Dictionaries of foreign languages are of two types. Firstly,
there are those which, generally written and published in
the native country, are the foreign equivalents to the English dictionaries we have just considered. Notable examples
are, in French, those of LITTRÉ and LAROUSSE (an encyclopaedic dictionary), and, in German, that of GRIMM.

Secondly, there are those (bi-lingual or multi-lingual)
designed to show the words of equivalent meaning in two,

or more, languages, e.g. English-German, English-French, Latin-English, Italian-Russian, etc.

It is impossible to mention specific examples here (see MINTO and MUDGE), but one matter should be stressed. The inquirer is apt to confine his attention to the bi-lingual type. Since, however, it may be difficult to be certain when using, say, an English-French dictionary whether you choose the correct one of the alternatives given (and if you select the wrong one, ridiculous results may ensue), it is wise, when in doubt, to turn to a good *French* dictionary where you will find explanations and examples which will remove all possibility of mistake.

As technical and commercial terms are often not included in the general dictionaries the following are invaluable:

> PITMAN'S TECHNICAL DICTIONARY OF ENGINEERING AND INDUSTRIAL SCIENCE IN SEVEN LANGUAGES, 4 vols., 1928-29,
>
> THE SCHLOMANN-OLDENBURG ILLUSTRATED TECHNICAL DICTIONARIES IN SIX LANGUAGES, 17 vols,
>
> A. WEBEL'S GERMAN-ENGLISH TECHNICAL AND SCIENTIFIC DICTIONARY,

and

> J. O. KETTRIDGE'S FRENCH-ENGLISH AND ENGLISH-FRENCH DICTIONARY OF COMMERCIAL AND FINANCIAL TERMS, PHRASES AND PRACTICE.

The above are bi-lingual or multi-lingual, but, as this is a scientifically and mechanically minded age, may we note some dictionaries of English and American terms (including also foreign words and phrases in use in this country).

The most recent are

> CHAMBERS'S TECHNICAL DICTIONARY,
>
> F. S. CRISPIN'S DICTIONARY OF TECHNICAL TERMS,
>
> H. BENNETT'S STANDARD CHEMICAL AND TECHNICAL DICTIONARY,

and

> F. D. JONES'S ENGINEERING ENCYCLOPAEDIA.

Others, published not long before the war, are

HUTCHINSON'S TECHNICAL AND SCIENTIFIC ENCYCLO-
PAEDIA,

OLIVER AND BOYD'S DICTIONARY OF SCIENTIFIC TERMS,

VAN NOSTRAND'S SCIENTIFIC ENCYCLOPEDIA,

J. G. HORNER'S DICTIONARY OF TERMS USED IN THE
THEORY AND PRACTICE OF MECHANICAL ENGINEERING,

and

C. M. BEADNELL'S DICTIONARY OF SCIENTIFIC TERMS.

Dictionaries and encyclopaedias are the most 'general' of
all books, in the sense that everyone, no matter what his
pursuits may be, must use them frequently. The next class
of book, however, is of little less wide appeal. We refer to
annuals or *year-books* – compact, concise compendia of information, particularly such as is of current value and deals
with recent events and the conditions of the present. The
outstanding example is

WHITAKER'S ALMANACK.

No other single small volume contains so much information of general interest. There are well over one thousand
octavo pages, but the facts are extraordinarily well selected
and condensed. On the title page we are told that it contains 'an account of the astronomical and other phenomena
and a vast amount of information respecting the government, finances, population, commerce and general statistics
of the various nations of the world', but that is only a rough
indication of what we shall find there. There is a dictionary
of abbreviations, particulars of the anniversaries of every
day of the year, an excellent survey of astronomy, high-
water and tide tables, a peerage, baronetage and knightage,
legal notes, details of professional fees, lists of hospitals,
parks, clubs, banks, insurance companies, salaries and wages
tables, weights and measures, sporting records, customs
tariffs, excise duties, taxes and, indeed, there is up-to-date
information on innumerable different matters. The index
contains thirty-five thousand entries – some indication of
the ground covered. The full, bound edition includes also
articles on questions of the day and annual summaries of

31

the year's work in science, invention, literature, art, music, drama, the films, broadcasting, etc. If there is any one book which everyone should know, and should have on his own shelves, it is WHITAKER'S ALMANACK.

An important American publication,

THE WORLD ALMANAC,

gives similar information, with special reference to the United States.

Even wider in scope, especially as regards information about countries other than Great Britain and the United States, are the three volumes of the Europa Service:

EUROPA: ENCYCLOPAEDIA OF EUROPE, 2 vols.,

and

ORBIS: ENCYCLOPAEDIA OF EXTRA-EUROPEAN STUDIES.

These are loose-leaf books kept up to date by the insertion of additional and revised pages. The arrangement – alphabetical by countries – is very convenient.

Neither should we overlook

THE STATESMAN'S YEAR BOOK,

a concise and reliable manual of statistical, descriptive, and historical information about all the countries of the world (the lists of official and unofficial publications dealing with each country are very useful), and

THE ANNUAL REGISTER,

a review of public events at home and abroad for the year, together with retrospects of literature, science and art, finance and commerce, law, obituary, etc. It has been issued every year since 1758 and consequently the complete set is invaluable to students of history.

In addition to these more or less general annuals, there are year-books dealing with most of the separate countries, e.g.

THE CANADA YEAR BOOK,

THE NEW ZEALAND OFFICIAL YEAR BOOK.

THE SOUTH AMERICAN HANDBOOK, etc. etc.

In the next chapter we shall deal with other reference books more limited in scope, because of either their subject or their form of presentation, but before passing on, one or two matters concerning *all* reference works should be stressed.

Firstly, nothing will save you so much time as a thorough knowledge of the most important works and of those to which, because of your individual needs, you will have most occasion to turn. Spend a few minutes, now and then, examining them; study the lists of contents. You will soon learn what you are likely to find in each and *vice versa*.

In particular, notice those features in each book which you might not *expect* to find there. For example, you have a dictionary and know that the bulk of it consists of the usual alphabetical list of words. Yet often between those two covers there are many other features of considerable utility. A dictionary in the possession of the writer contains also a good atlas of the world and a descriptive account of the various countries, a universal almanack, thirty-three columns of additional words, a dictionary of proper names running into one hundred and fifty pages, a glossary of foreign words and phrases, a guide to correct usage, a long list of disputed spellings and pronunciations, a dictionary of abbreviations and contractions and a list of signs and symbols used in science, commerce and typography, and, most amusing and unexpected, a list showing the symbolism of flowers and gems.

A casual user might easily overlook this additional information and spend time searching for it elsewhere, when all the while it was ready to hand.

To give a more specialized instance:

THE PUBLIC SCHOOLS YEAR-BOOK

is essentially 'a list of the public secondary schools represented on the Headmasters' Conference', but over two hundred and fifty pages, approximately a quarter of the whole, are devoted to entrance into and education for the principal professions and careers, on which matter it is probably the best existing guide.

Secondly, though for most of the larger reference books

you must go to your library, you should have, in your own home and office, a collection of the smaller works needed most frequently. A comparatively small private reference library, if well selected, will answer many of your questions, and it will answer them without trouble or delay when and where the difficulty arises.

This home, or office, library should at least include the following: a small encyclopaedia, an English dictionary, perhaps also English-French, English-German and English-Latin dictionaries, WHITAKER'S ALMANACK, a biographical dictionary, a gazetteer and atlas, a local directory, and a railway time-table. To these general works add those of especial importance in relation to your work or hobbies.

The household library can also with advantage include two or three of the more popular type of reference book, such as

PEARS' ANNUAL,

which is, within its scope, a really admirable compendium of useful information on a great variety of topics, and is very cheap; and

THE DAILY MAIL YEAR BOOK,

a kind of Whitaker, much less thorough, but not without its uses.

There should be some library, large or small, wherever work is done. Books are the tools of the worker, whatever the trade or business. Yet it is surprising how deficient some offices and workshops are in this respect. Our larger industrial and commercial concerns often maintain excellent up-to-date research libraries, some employing trained librarians to administer them. Such provision is impossible and unnecessary in most instances, but even the smallest office is definitely not properly equipped if it lacks dictionaries, gazetteers, atlases, standard textbooks on the business and its operation, law, etc., books of tables, calculations and formulae, the most-used directories, and so on.

There is always the public library in the background ready to help the business inquirer, but obviously it is much more convenient to have as much data as can be conveniently and economically provided ready to hand on the premises.

It is not, of course, always necessary to *go* to the library (if your own books do not meet the situation). The central library in your town is sure to be on the telephone, and if the inquiry is one which can be answered briefly the library staff will be happy to give you the required information, by 'phone and without charge, as quickly as possible. When you do this (unless you are definitely told to 'hold on') do not wait, as often an apparently simple query takes longer to answer than was anticipated. Give your telephone number; the library will call you when the facts are available.

Though *all* types of question are referred to the library, the most frequent demands are for addresses, definitions, places, distances, etc., which the smaller office books do not provide. Clearly, to mention the first alone, only firms with widespread connections would be justified in purchasing up-to-date directories of the whole country; when the need arises they phone or send a messenger to the library; but they would not dream of relying upon the library for local directories and, similarly, it is wasteful to depend on it for everyday data which could be housed on a single shelf.

Our information service, like charity, should begin at home.

The above remark, however, is not intended to deter readers from making the fullest use of the public library service – on the contrary, it is meant only to remind them of the convenience of having the more generally needed data ready to hand. You must never forget the library, whether you need books or facts, and you should never hesitate to use it.

One library has issued a small poster bearing the words: 'Whenever you want to know anything ask the Public Library to help you'. Copies are displayed in works and offices where they will serve as a constant reminder. The advice is sound.

Remember – though some of this is a repetition of remarks made elsewhere in these pages it is sufficiently important to demand emphasis – that the public library has unique facilities for the collection and dissemination of information, that the staff are expert fact-finders, that they do not care a rap what you want or why and will never ask any questions, that they will treat all your inquiries as confidential, that they will never regard any question as too trivial, that they want to be of service to all who seek their help, and that no charge is ever made for any such assistance.

CHAPTER THREE

MORE QUESTION-ANSWERING
BOOKS

BEFORE they saw the names in the last chapter, how many readers of this book had ever heard of Ephraim Chambers, or John Harris, or Coronelli – even of Pliny the Elder? Yet they did much for the benefit of future generations. As a rule we are not ungenerous in praising our benefactors, be they scientists, explorers, statesmen or thinkers, but perhaps, because their work was not romantic or spectacular, we forget many to whom we are indebted and take their gifts for granted. Dictionaries, encyclopaedias, maps – all the time-saving, knowledge-preserving compilations we are now considering – were invented and perfected by clever and infinitely painstaking men who cannot have had much thought for fame and fortune so long as their work would be useful. Is it not fair, therefore, that we should sometimes pause to recollect that they who make knowledge available are little less our benefactors than the discoverers and pioneers? Hence this little interlude.

As we have ventured to interpolate one digression may we make another – dealing with a very important point which must be mentioned somewhere in this book. It is this: We tell you in these pages about some of the thousands of reference books that exist for your benefit; we say little about those that *don't* exist, but every librarian could list dozens of subjects for which up-to-date sources of information are lacking. Remember, however, that good accurate reference books are difficult and expensive to compile. They embody the work of experts over periods of many years. Moreover, they are expensive to publish; think, for example, how much longer it must take to put into type the closely-packed page of a bi-lingual dictionary than the easy-running, comfortably spaced page of an ordinary novel or biography. Yet some, perhaps most, reference books are necessarily limited in appeal and consequently in 'sales'. It is, indeed, true that publishers will often take considerable risks, both for the 'prestige' value of such publications and because they genuinely desire to make a worthy contribution to knowledge, but on the whole publishers and compilers must consider the likelihood of adequate sales. So the only way we can encourage the publication of new works of reference, and up-to-date editions of existing ones, is to make the fullest use of those we have, to buy as many as we can usefully add to our home and office libraries and to ask for others at our public libraries so that librarians in turn may be justified in providing a yet wider selection.

To return to our main theme, however, let us next consider some further 'general' reference books – those which, though still of wide appeal, deal with cross-sections of knowledge.

From the beginning it was inevitable that some kind of specialization was needed. No general book could comprise everything. Our Chinaman, with his five thousand volumes, seems to have tried to embrace as much as he could, but all other reference books are selective. There is a limit, firstly, to what an editor or even a large staff can achieve in a lifetime, and secondly, to the size of the publication, which, after a point, must cease to be convenient. To go beyond that limit – to attain any real measure of completeness – the compiler had to mark off a definite field and confine himself within it. He had either to choose a special subject or branch of knowledge, such as engineering, the Bible, or Greek pottery, or he had to select one aspect only of general things, such as the people or the places or the events concerned, thus selecting only one of the many factors in the general encyclopaedia. In the next chapter we shall consider books limited by subject; in this let us discuss the second type mentioned above.

For information about *people* – who they were (or are), what they did, when they lived – we turn to *biographical dictionaries*, of which there are three main types: (*a*) general ones covering the men and women of all times and all nations, (*b*) those limited to the people of one country, and (*c*) those confined to special classes – actors, scientists, soldiers, authors, etc. Furthermore, we have those which deal with men of the past (or of the past *and* the present) and those limited to living people. At this point it should be noted that much biographical information (and also information concerning places, dates, etc.) is to be found in general encyclopaedias and the like. When seeking for such data always adopt the golden rule of looking first in the most likely and the most accessible sources. Encyclopaedias will give you the most important facts about the most notable personages; if that is what you want, and if the encyclopaedia is handiest, try it first. But if the person is of lesser importance, or if you want detailed data, go straightway to the best available biographical dictionary and, especially, to the one which is most likely to deal thoroughly with people of his nationality or profession. In other words, unless the general work is so much more handy that it is worth while trying it, go at once to the most specialized and detailed book to which you have ready access.

To return – the handiest of general biographical dictionaries is

CHAMBERS'S BIOGRAPHICAL DICTIONARY,

a comprehensive, though relatively not very detailed, work.

NELSON'S BIOGRAPHICAL DICTIONARY

is smaller but similar in scope.

SIR J. A. HAMMERTON'S CONCISE UNIVERSAL BIOGRAPHY, published, like the two just cited, not long before the war, embraces 20,000 famous men and women of all nations and times and includes a great many portraits, mostly small.

A larger, American, work (though its *scope* is international) is

LIPPINCOTT'S PRONOUNCING DICTIONARY OF BIOGRAPHY
AND MYTHOLOGY.

For brief data do not forget the CENTURY CYCLOPÆDIA OF
NAMES, already mentioned.

A. D. HYAMSON'S DICTIONARY OF UNIVERSAL BIOGRAPHY,
1916,

is useful because it includes thousands of persons not included elsewhere, but it gives only the briefest information
– name, birth and death dates, and what he or she was, all
in one line per person.

There is, indeed, room for a really good, full, and
comprehensive general biographical dictionary, for though
the general encyclopaedias and the national and subject
dictionaries mentioned below cover the ground very
thoroughly, it is often necessary to look in several places
before being satisfied.

The field of *national biography* is much better provided.
For example, in

THE DICTIONARY OF NATIONAL BIOGRAPHY, 63 vols.,
with three supplements bringing the work down to 1921
(with indexes, etc., making 73 vols. in all) we have a fine,
authoritative and complete record of English men and
women (including Americans of the Colonial period) of all
times and in all spheres of activity. The D.N.B. – to adopt
the usual brief designation – is comprehensive in a double
sense of the word because, while very few names are
omitted, really full details are given of all the more notable
people. The length of the biographies is, roughly, propor-
tionate to the importance of the people described, and the
longer articles run to several pages. Much information is to
be found in the D.N.B. which is quite unobtainable any-
where else, while full references to other sources, details of
the person's own publications, and sometimes information
regarding portraits, are given. Living people are not
included.

The D.N.B. may be seen at most fair-sized libraries,
while the single volume INDEX AND EPITOME, which gives

condensed biographies of all the people included in the main work and the first supplement (i.e. to 1901), will prove a useful addition to the home library.

A useful supplement to the D.N.B. is

FREDERICK BOASE'S MODERN ENGLISH BIOGRAPHY, 6 vols., 1892-1921,

as it includes some thousands of less-well-known men who are *not* included in the larger work, but it is limited to those who have died since 1850.

A similar publication to the D.N.B., but dealing with American celebrities, is

THE DICTIONARY OF AMERICAN BIOGRAPHY, 20 vols., 1928-37.

For living people we turn to

WHO'S WHO,

an annual volume embracing most of the outstanding contemporary Englishmen as well as a few foreigners. Full details of career, publications, appointments, degrees, etc., are given, with usually some personal facts such as 'hobbies'. Addresses and clubs are generally mentioned.

A companion publication, issued every few years, is

WHO WAS WHO,

which includes the entries for those who, previously figuring in WHO'S WHO, have since died. It is a useful link between the D.N.B. and the current WHO'S WHO, and should not be overlooked.

WHO'S WHO IN AMERICA

is similar; there is also a WHO WAS WHO IN AMERICA embracing people who died between 1837 and 1941.

Since 1940 the American H. W. Wilson Co. has issued

CURRENT BIOGRAPHY

monthly, with annual cumulations – very useful for men and women who have recently come into prominence or 'got into the news'.

Before the war there were several other national 'who's whos', such as the French QUI ÊTES-VOUS? the Italian CHI É and the Dutch WIE IS DAT? Doubtless new editions of these and similar works will soon be available again. There is also an

INTERNATIONAL WHO'S WHO

published by the Europa Service.

For members of the titled and landed classes we have recourse to

BURKE'S GENERAL AND HERALDIC HISTORY OF THE PEERAGE AND BARONETAGE, THE PRIVY COUNCIL AND KNIGHTAGE,

DEBRETT'S PEERAGE, BARONETAGE, KNIGHTAGE AND COMPANIONAGE,

and

BURKE'S LANDED GENTRY.

Shorter and cheaper books of this type are DOD'S PEERAGE, WHITAKER'S PEERAGE, BARONETAGE, KNIGHTAGE AND COMPANIONAGE, and KELLY'S HANDBOOK TO THE TITLED, LANDED AND OFFICIAL CLASSES.

For Members of Parliament see

DOD'S PARLIAMENTARY COMPANION

and

VACHER'S PARLIAMENTARY COMPANION.

Biographical dictionaries and Who's Whos confined to special professions are so numerous that detailed mention is impossible. A few typical examples are WHO'S WHO IN THE THEATRE, WHO'S WHO IN LITERATURE, CROCKFORD'S CLERICAL DIRECTORY, THE MEDICAL DIRECTORY, and THE CATHOLIC WHO'S WHO. A few others are mentioned in the next chapter, and lists of others are given in MINTO'S REFERENCE BOOKS, MUDGE'S GUIDE TO REFERENCE BOOKS (and its supplements) – already mentioned – in HIRSHBERG'S SUBJECT GUIDE TO REFERENCE BOOKS, and in L. R. and E. R. MCCOLVIN'S LIBRARY STOCK AND ASSISTANCE TO READERS – all books to which we must keep on referring as they cover so much of the ground of this present little volume. See also the brief

A.S.L.I.B. CLASSIFIED LIST OF ANNUALS AND YEAR BOOKS.

If you are interested in any special profession, say,

architects, local government officials, sportsmen, etc., inquire whether special Who's Whos exist.

Do not forget that separate autobiographies, biographies, memoirs and volumes of reminiscences have been written about and by most of the noteworthy people of the past and, to some extent, the present. For these you must ask at your library and consult the various catalogues and biblio-graphies mentioned in a later chapter.

There are also numerous collections of short biographies in book form and in periodicals, so if you cannot find a full-length biography there might be a briefer account in one of these. To trace it use

P. M. RICHES' ANALYTICAL BIBLIOGRAPHY OF UNIVERSAL
COLLECTED BIOGRAPHY, 1934.

Often we want not only information, but also portraits of those in whom we are interested, and these are some-times difficult to obtain. The obvious first step is to see whether their lives have been written, since most bio-graphies include at least one portrait. If this is not the case, try

THE A.L.A. (AMERICAN LIBRARY ASSOCIATION) PORTRAIT
INDEX, 1906,

which analyses over six thousand volumes and shows where some one hundred and twenty thousand portraits of nearly forty-five thousand different people are to be found.

HISTORICAL PORTRAITS, 1400-1850, 4 vols., 1909-1919, is not an index, but a collection of actual portraits of the great English men and women of nearly five centuries, very well reproduced and provided with short biographical notes.

Another and very comprehensive series of portraits, though they are very small and not too well printed, is embraced in the 'picture encyclopaedia',

I SEE ALL, 5 vols.,

which is an alphabetical series of one hundred thousand pictures of all manner of things, places and people. As before said, they are merely miniatures, but good enough to serve many needs.

Dictionaries of places, showing where they are situated and perhaps giving information as to population, industries, notable features, etc., are called *gazetteers*.

The most recent are

CASSELL'S WORLD PICTORIAL GAZETTEER,

with 1500 small maps and illustrations, and

NELSON'S WORLD GAZETTEER AND GEOGRAPHICAL
DICTIONARY,

which contains also sixty-four pages of maps and is a handy desk book of nearly six hundred pages. World gazetteers on a larger scale are

LIPPINCOTT'S NEW GAZETTEER, 1906 (reprinted with
supplement in 1922), and

LONGMAN'S GAZETTEER OF THE WORLD, 1902.

As will be seen, neither of these is really up to date, but they are still useful, since, apart from population data and changes in place names, there is not much to get out of date. London and Slocum-on-Puddle are still where they were in 1902. Furthermore, once you have discovered the country and district in which a place is situated, it is not difficult to obtain recent information from guide-books, year-books and the like. In passing, remember that the indexes to guide-books (if you know the approximate location) can be made to serve as gazetteers; the more thorough guide-books include plenty of smaller places not listed in gazetteers.

The best gazetteers of this country are

BARTHOLOMEW'S SURVEY GAZETTEER OF THE BRITISH
ISLES, 9th edn., 1943,

BRADSHAW'S RAILWAY AND COMMERCIAL GAZETTEER OF
ENGLAND, SCOTLAND AND WALES,

and

PHILIP'S HANDY GAZETTEER OF THE BRITISH ISLES.

Though they usually only give location, the indexes to atlases of the world or of the different countries (see Chapter Six) are invaluable.

To find out *when* anything occurred we can turn to such

dictionaries of dates, chronologies, and similar historical works as

HAYDN'S DICTIONARY OF DATES AND UNIVERSAL INFOR-
MATION, 1910.

This embraces historical, political, ecclesiastical, legal, social, commercial, scientific, literary, artistic and other events, a valuable feature being the lists given under various headings, e.g. abdications, assassinations, conspiracies, planets, Lord Mayors, bishops, etc., while useful chronological summaries of the history of all countries are provided.

NELSON'S DICTIONARY OF DATES

is more recent, and in twelve hundred small pages comprises a mass of data.

Another, a volume in Everyman's Library, is a DICTIONARY OF DATES, revised edition, 1940.

Much the most general and detailed, however, are HELEN R. KELLER'S DICTIONARY OF DATES, based upon Haydn, and C. E. LITTLE'S CYCLOPÆDIA OF CLASSIFIED DATES, 1900, where dates are arranged first by country, then chronologically, each period being further subdivided for army and navy, art, science, births and deaths, church, letters, society, state, etc., and detailed indexes are provided. An American work, it is unfortunately out of print and difficult to obtain.

On the whole, inquirers may find these rather less useful than other types of reference books – probably because the ground to be covered is so immense and because it is more difficult to make a selection of the most useful facts. Therefore, direct recourse to standard historical and biographical books, special subject reference works, etc., is often quicker.

There are also a few 'chronologies' and dictionaries of history (see next chapter) and in 1935 the Encyclopædia Britannica Co. published an unusual volume called

THE MARCH OF MAN,

'a chronological record of peoples and events from prehistoric times to the present day, comprising a comparative time chart of universal history', an historical atlas and many illustrations.

We pass next to *directories*. No reference books, except perhaps time-tables, are better known to the general public, and so no description is necessary. Their range is wide. The famous firm of Kelly's Directories Ltd. publishes separate volumes for the big cities such as London, Liverpool, Birmingham, etc., for all the English counties, and for most of the London suburban districts, as well as a series devoted to separate trades e.g.,

 THE BUILDING TRADES DIRECTORY,

 THE CABINET, FURNISHING AND UPHOLSTERY TRADES
  DIRECTORY, etc.,

and a very fine

 DIRECTORY OF MERCHANTS, MANUFACTURERS AND
  SHIPPERS OF THE WORLD.

This gives much useful gazetteer information, a glossary of trade terms, a trade marks section, etc.

In addition there are various local publications of varying importance, and several commercial directories, of which STUBBS' is a good example. Lists of directories are given in CANNON'S CLASSIFIED GUIDE TO 1,700 ANNUALS, and in WILLING'S PRESS GUIDE.

The larger public libraries carry a fairly complete range; nearly all take those covering the immediate district, the London directory, and a few commercial ones.

Our chief reason for mentioning directories here, however, is to draw attention to the fact that they are often much more than mere lists of names and addresses. Each of the famous county directories published by Kelly, for example, is, in the words of one of the prefaces, in some measure also a gazetteer, giving a full topographical account of every town, parish, village and township, and descriptions of the principal buildings and objects of interest. Full information is given as to county councils; the Hundreds and County Court Districts; the Cathedral; the churches (with the value of the livings and the names of the patrons and incumbents); the chief landowners, with details as to the principal seats; the hospitals; the acreage, soil and crops; the markets and fairs; the means of conveyance, etc., while articles on the geology of the county with sketch maps, and a good general map, are also included.

Nowadays, when so many people are on the telephone, the

TELEPHONE DIRECTORY

is a good partial substitute for an expensive set of ordinary directories, and a complete series of telephone directories, covering the whole of Great Britain, can be bought for a few shillings. Addresses and businesses or professions are, of course, given. Many libraries which cannot afford all the county books have the telephone directory, which has the advantage, often, of being more up to date, since, whereas the county directories are only issued every three years or so, the telephone directories are published every six months.

Yet a further value of the telephone directory lies in the fact that it includes many people who do not appear in the ordinary ones. These latter usually mention the householder, while many who are in flats or lodgings, or perhaps are relations of the householders, figure in the telephone book.

There are also *directories of telegraphic addresses* (e.g. MARCONI'S INTERNATIONAL REGISTER OF TELEGRAPHIC AND TRADE ADDRESSES, and SELL'S DIRECTORY OF REGISTERED TELEGRAPHIC ADDRESSES), while the larger libraries are usually provided with the standard telegraphic code books.

Lastly, our everyday demands will call for some *dictionary of quotations* or other. Not only do we often need to ensure that a phrase is being quoted correctly, or to discover who wrote it and in which of his works it appears; dictionaries of quotations are useful in suggesting appropriate expressions for use in speeches, essays and the like, and they provide good and thought-provoking reading matter for odd moments.

Probably the best for general purposes are

W. GURNEY BENHAM'S NEW BOOK OF QUOTATIONS, 1929,

J. A. BARTLETT'S FAMILIAR QUOTATIONS,

and

THE OXFORD DICTIONARY OF QUOTATIONS,

Three good American works are

H. L. MENCKEN'S A NEW DICTIONARY OF QUOTATIONS,

B. E. STEVENSON'S HOME DICTIONARY OF QUOTATIONS,

and

J. K. HOYT'S NEW ENCYCLOPEDIA OF PRACTICAL QUOTA-
TIONS.

There is also a smaller DICTIONARY OF QUOTATIONS in Everyman's Library of which a completely new edition is in preparation.

These all include some quotations from foreign authors, but fuller lists are given in the series of volumes published some years ago by Allen & Unwin: FRENCH QUOTATIONS, by HARBOTTLE AND DALBIAC; GERMAN, by DALBIAC; ITALIAN, by HARBOTTLE AND DALBIAC; SPANISH, by HARBOTTLE AND HUME; and ORIENTAL (ARABIC AND PERSIAN), by FIELD.

See also

H. P. JONES'S DICTIONARY OF FOREIGN PHRASES AND
CLASSICAL QUOTATIONS

with English translations or equivalents.

In addition, there are numerous dictionaries and concordances of the works of individual authors (see MINTO, MUDGE and MCCOLVIN'S LIBRARY STOCK).

When selecting a dictionary of quotations for purchase, note firstly what field is covered (e.g. if you are especially interested in modern literature, a book is useless for your purpose if it excludes living authors), and secondly, whether full reference to the book (or play, or poem) stating the chapter, act, verse or even line, is made. Some dictionaries only give the author's name, which, in nine cases out of ten, is most unsatisfactory; you know *that* much already.

For proverbs see

G. L. APPERSON'S ENGLISH PROVERBS AND PROVERBIAL
PHRASES,

an historical dictionary.

CHAPTER FOUR

REFERENCE BOOKS FOR SPECIAL SUBJECTS

WHATEVER your pursuits may be you will have to use most of the books so far described; they are the fundamental sources of information, valuable alike to the school teacher, the business man, the preacher, the scientist, the young student, and the housewife. Most of us, however, specialize in some branch of activity, and consequently many of our questions will fall within a fairly well-defined field – it may be education, religion, psychology, or what not. For all the principal branches of study and inquiry, special reference guides exist.

The next step in your education in the art of finding out is, therefore, to make yourself acquainted with the most important special reference works on your own particular subject. There are so many really important publications – *how* important you cannot estimate until you have tested them fully – and the needs of readers of this book will be so varied, that it is difficult to cover this phase of our theme at all satisfactorily.

In the following pages, however, you will find a list of one hundred typical reference books on a wide variety of subjects and of many types. Fuller lists are to be found in the books by MINTO, MUDGE, HIRSHBERG and MCCOLVIN, to which you have already been referred several times, and in others mentioned in HOW TO USE BOOKS. *This* list is given for three reasons. Firstly, the works listed are all so definitely useful that every inquirer interested in each particular subject *should* know them; maybe he already uses them regularly, but if not he will surely be glad to have them brought to his notice – for example, no music lover would willingly ignore GROVE'S DICTIONARY OF MUSIC, no engineer KEMPE'S ENGINEERS' YEAR-BOOK. Secondly, the list will, within its limits, show the general inquirer where to turn next when general books fail. Thirdly, those who are concerned with some topic *not* listed will naturally ask whether there are not similar books to help *them* and so set about discovering guides to their own subjects.

Every book listed below is reasonably accessible; most, if not all, are in every good public library. If they are not in *your* library, suggest that they be obtained. To save space, the briefest possible titles are given.

Accounting: Pixley's Accountants' Dictionary.

Advertising: Pitman's Dictionary of Advertising and Printing.

Art: Bryan's Dictionary of Painters and Engravers.

Hourticq's Encyclopedia of Art.

The Year's Art.

Banking and Finance: Brook's Concise Dictionary of Finance.

Thomson's Dictionary of Banking.

Bible: Hastings' Dictionary of the Bible.

Hastings' Dictionary of Christ and the Gospels.

Cruden's Complete Concordance.

Young's Analytical Concordance.

Gore's New Commentary.

Botany: Sowerby's English Botany.

Business and Commerce: Pitman's Business Man's Encyclopaedia and Dictionary of Commerce.

Pitman's Dictionary of Secretarial Law and Practice.

Building: Laxton's Builders' Price Book.

Specification.

Catholicism (Roman): The Catholic Encyclopaedia.

Charities, etc.: Annual Charities Register.

Burdett's Hospitals and Charities.

Chemical Technology: Thorpe's Dictionary of Applied Chemistry.

Church of England: Ollard's Dictionary of English Church History.

Crockford's Clerical Directory.

Clocks: Britten's Old Clocks and Watches.
Cricket: Wisden's Cricketers' Almanac.
Customs and Manners: Chambers's Book of Days.
  Hutchinson's Customs of the World.
Domestic Economy: Black's Domestic Dictionary.
  Beeton's Book of Household Management.
  Enquire Within upon Everything.
Economics: Palgrave's Dictionary of Political Economy.
Education: Monroe's Cyclopedia of Education.
  Pitman's Encyclopaedia and Dictionary of Education.
  Girls' School Year Book.
Engineering: Kempe's Engineers' Year-Book.
  Fowler's Mechanical Engineers' Pocket Book.
  Fowler's Electrical Engineer's Handbook.
  Machinery's Handbook.
Engravings: Slater's Engravings and their Value.
Films: Kinematograph Year Book.
  International Motion Picture Almanack.
Flags: Gordon's Flags of the World.
Furniture: Macquoid's Dictionary of English Furniture.
Games (Indoor): Foster's Complete Hoyle.
Gardening: Black's Gardening Dictionary.
  Coutts' Complete Book of Gardening.
  Wright's Encyclopaedia of Gardening.
Gold and Silver Ware: Chaffer's Hall Marks on Gold and
    Silver Plate.
  Jackson's English Goldsmiths and their Marks.
Heraldry, etc.: Fox-Davies' Art of Heraldry.
  Fox-Davies' Book of Public Arms.
  Fairbairn's Book of Crests.
History: Brendon's Dictionary of British History.
  Low and Pulling's Dictionary of English History.
  Langer's Encyclopaedia of World History.
Hymns: Julian's Dictionary of Hymnology.
Jews and Judaism: The Jewish Encyclopaedia.
Law for the Layman: Everyman's Own Lawyer.
  Stone's Justices Manual.

Literature: Brewer's Dictionary of Phrase and Fable.
Brewer's Readers' Handbook.
Keller's Readers' Digest of Books.
Chambers's Cyclopaedia of English Literature.
Magnus's Dictionary of European Literature.

Local Government: Local Government Manual.
Municipal Year-Book.

London: Cunningham's London.
Harben's Dictionary of London.
Kent's Encyclopaedia of London.

Medicine: Black's Medical Dictionary.
Baker and Margerison's New Medical Dictionary.
Medical Directory.

Mohammedanism: The Encyclopaedia of Islam.

Music: Grove's Dictionary of Music and Musicians.
The International Cyclopædia of Music and Musicians.
Black's Dictionary of Music and Musicians.
Kobbé's Complete Opera Book.
Hinrichsen's Music Year Book.

Mythology: Edwardes' Dictionary of Non-Classical Mythology.
Grey's Mythology of All Races.
Lemprière's Classical Dictionary.
Smith's Smaller Classical Dictionary.

Philosophy and Psychology: Baldwin's Dictionary of Philosophy and Psychology.
Warren's Dictionary of Psychology.

Photography: Wall's Dictionary of Photography.

Physics: Glazebrook's Dictionary of Applied Physics.

Pottery and Porcelain: Chaffer's Marks and Monographs on European and Oriental Pottery and Porcelain.
Burton and Hobson's Handbook of Marks on Pottery and Porcelain.

Poultry: Suttie's Dictionary of Poultry.

Religion: Hastings' Encyclopaedia of Religion and Ethics.

Sociology: Seligman's Encyclopaedia of the Social Sciences.

Stamp Collecting: Stanley Gibbons' Priced Catalogue.
 Whitfield King's Standard Catalogue.
Statistics: Mulhall's Dictionary of Statistics.
 Webb's New Dictionary of Statistics.
Stocks and Shares: Stock Exchange Year-Book.
 Directory of Directors.
Technology, etc.: Henley's 20th Century Formulas, Recipes
 and Processes.
 Spon's Workshop Receipts.
 The Scientific American Cyclopædia of Formulas.
Wireless: The B.B.C. Year-Book.

So far the inquirer's path is fairly straightforward. He takes his questions to books designed to answer them. When he has acquired a little experience in handling these quickly, and when he has found out which will serve him and where they are located on the library shelves, a wealth of data is at his command.

When 'handling' books the inexperienced waste much time. They open dictionaries at random and start turning over the pages patiently until they find the right one, and then wade slowly through it from beginning to end for the required word. This is unnecessary. With practice it is easy to estimate whereabouts, within a few pages, to open the closed volume and then to judge how many more pages to turn either back or forward. One really does a little mental arithmetic: if the whole alphabet occupies the entire volume of, say, six hundred pages, or a thickness of three inches, you may estimate that, having regard for the differing bulk of the various words, letter T will come half-an-inch from the back, and so on. Some dictionaries are provided with thumb indexes. Nearly all reference books have headlines indicating the exact scope of each page. Use these aids to speed. If a book is *not* arranged alphabetically, go straight to the index or the table of contents. It **is** astonishing how many people try to 'find' what they want for several minutes before they think of the index.

When the work is in several volumes the compass of each is often indicated on the back outside (e.g. Vol. 1, A – D, or Vol. 5, 1763-1802). If this is not done, try to remember where each volume ends and so avoid continually pulling the wrong volumes down from the shelves. These are little points, but in the long run they save time.

Up to now we have dealt only with books intended for reference purposes. Once, however, the inquirer has found that these more obvious items do not answer his questions he must enter the wider realm of general literature, and he may find this bewildering in its profusion and complexity.

A method of approach is essential.

First of all, have recourse to those books which are most accessible; that is to say, first try your own books, if at all likely, then go to your local library, and then, if necessary, try to find out if there are *other* books not in your library, but which you may be able to obtain. This may seem very obvious, but the writer, in his occupation as public librarian, has more than once gone to some trouble to secure special books at the request of readers who, on receiving them, have found them useless, and have then disclosed their *actual* needs. It has often happened that had the writer known these in the first instance he could have provided the necessary information in five minutes from books in his own library.

Work from the most likely to the least likely, from the most accessible to the least accessible – let it be repeated.

Supposing you have tried your own books and then go to the library. You have there two alternatives – either to say to the assistant in the Reference Department that you want to know the annual production of peanuts in Patagonia (or whatever your query may be), or to try and find out for yourself from the available books.

Frankly, the first plan is usually the best; the staff of a good library will willingly take whatever steps are necessary to provide the information, even going beyond the bounds of their own printed sources if need be, and they can always do the job much quicker than you could do it.

But, on the other hand, yours might not be a good library, suitably staffed for information service, and moreover, in the course of solving one problem you may learn a great deal of value about other things. So let us see how you should set about your inquiry for yourself.

(a) The obvious reference books have been tried.

(b) What is the 'subject' of your inquiry? To what main department of knowledge does it belong? Define it as closely as possible. For example, it is an aspect of engineering, of locomotive engineering, of boilers; it is an historical matter, French history, seventeenth century. By so 'classifying' it you narrow down the field in which to search, and so put on one side a mass of material in which it is *not* necessary, in the first instance at least, to look. Sometimes it is not easy to 'place' your inquiry like this; it seems to belong equally to two or more provinces of knowledge; note these alternatives and try them in turn.

(c) All public libraries, excepting the smallest and most inefficient, are classified according to some recognized system. Find out, from the subject index to the system, or by inquiry, the place on the shelves where books on locomotive boilers or seventeenth century French history are to be found. Examine the books there, commencing with those which seem most likely, most comprehensive, most authoritative and most up to date.

(d) You may conduct your inquiries in the reference department – indeed, such will usually be the case. Don't forget, however, that more, and often better, books on the same subject are shelved in the lending department. You will usually be allowed to go into the lending library to see these for yourself, even if you are not a registered borrower, or they may be brought into the reference library for you.

(e) If, under the specific heading, there is no book answering the question, try the more general subject (i.e. locomotive engineering and French history), or even the still wider topic (engineering, modern history). Usually the more general subjects are arranged *before* the subdivisions. That is to say, from the special to the general you work backwards (i.e. to your left on a shelf, from lower to higher shelves, and from the top shelf of one case to the bottom shelf of the case to its left). Always, in a big subject, allow for intervening subdivisions, e.g., before you come to general French history skip a few shelves (according to the size of the library) for sixteenth, fifteenth, etc., century sub-divisions.

(*f*) Consult the catalogues, as there may be other books which are (1) kept in storage to which the public has not access, or (2) in the hands of other readers. If you notice any at all likely books, in the first case ask for them, and in the second, if you can wait, ask for them to be reserved for you when they are returned to the library. Do not forget, also, that *all* the books may not be in *one* sequence; for example, larger books are usually shelved on suitable shelves at the end of each main class or in separate book cases.

(*g*) Think of other possible subjects which might cross your own at the point of inquiry. It is surprising how closely related most things are in this world. You may often find your information by approaching it from an angle. For instance, your boiler problem *might* – you must judge for yourself whether it is worth trying – be of interest to the physicist, or to the manufacturer of steel, or to the marine engineer; it might be described as an example to illustrate something fundamentally quite different. Your seventeenth-century France query might enter into a discussion of the constitutional history of France, or its economic history, or its colonial policy, or it might be mentioned in a biography of some prominent man of the time, or it might enter into a survey of the foreign relations of France with another country. Think and try. As you gain experience you will find yourself thinking more fruitfully and trying less hopelessly.

(*h*) If these steps fail, *in practice* you should *always* take your difficulty to the most senior library assistant on duty, telling him (to save his time) where you have looked. He may possibly suggest sources you have overlooked. Always tell him *exactly* what you want. 'Of course', you might remark. The writer knows from long experience, however, that perhaps a majority of inquirers, for some unknown reason, are reluctant to disclose their precise difficulty. The library assistant has to coax it out of them.

(*i*) However, in this survey of procedure you are presumed to be searching for yourself and so, if steps (*a*) to (*g*) fail you must turn to the various guides to literature described in the next chapter and – but further steps are discussed as we proceed.

Before leaving books, certain types call for special attention.

(1) About most subjects one or more really comprehensive standard treatises have been written. Although these are primarily surveys for the use of students, and the material is arranged according to the requirements of systematic study, most of them cover the ground so completely and are so well indexed that they are invaluable also as *reference* books. Always refer to them next after the more definitely reference works, if not in the first instance.

Examples are given, not only to indicate the type, but also because the books mentioned are worth bringing to the notice of all who do not already know them.

The Cambridge Ancient History.
The Cambridge Mediaeval History.
The Cambridge Modern History.
The Cambridge History of English Literature.
The Cambridge History of American Literature.
The Victoria History of the Counties of England.
Oman's History of England.
Hunt and Boole's Political History of England.
Ward's English Poets.
The Cambridge Natural History.

The Oxford History of Music.
Allen's Commercial Organic Analysis.
Mellor's Inorganic and Theoretical Chemistry.
Fortesque's History of the British Army, etc. etc.

(2) It is surprising how little the general reader makes use of the accurate and up-to-date information contained in the official publications of the Government and other authorities. Some years ago he dubbed them 'Blue Books', and decided that they were stodgy, unpleasant, and only fit for dreary statisticians. Actually, only a few are 'blue' in any sense of the word; most are stodgy only in that they are well compressed and condensed.

Official publications – both parliamentary papers prepared in the first instance for the use and information of both Houses, and those issued by the various Government Departments (comprehensively called Stationery Office Publications) – contain facts and figures relating to a great many matters of current importance. Undoubtedly hundreds of official documents are for purely departmental and record purposes, but others embrace data, unobtainable elsewhere, of value to business men, to all interested in economic and social conditions, to manufacturers, scientific workers, and, indeed, students of many matters.

This wide range is not generally appreciated. The Stationery Office issues a monthly list of publications as well as an annual consolidated list. Let us glance at the index to the latter and note some of the many matters about which up-to-date and authoritative information can be found: Pay as You Earn, Payment by Results, Pear Scab, Penicillin, Pensions, Physical Training, Planning our New Homes, Plastics, Plumbing, Plums and Damsons, Police, Population, Poultry Manure, Public Schools, Punishment for War Crimes and Pupils' Record Cards.

Before the war a valuable subject index,

GUIDE TO CURRENT OFFICIAL STATISTICS OF THE UNITED
KINGDOM

was published.

Catalogues of important Parliamentary Papers from 1801 have been published by Messrs. P. S. King & Son.

Though they are not so readily accessible, the specialist student should remember that the Governments of other countries publish similar, if less extensive, documents, while even local government authorities (such as the London County Council) issue useful publications from time to time.

United States Governments publications may now be obtained from and examined at the Stationery Office in London.

(3) The catalogues and handbooks of many museums and art galleries often serve a much wider purpose than that of merely listing the exhibits. The best embrace a wealth of general historical and descriptive information, and, especially when the actual collections are comprehensive, these books may be the very best guides for students of those particular subjects. Examine a few, such as the Victoria and Albert Museum catalogues of rings, of English porcelain, ironwork, lace, stained glass, English furniture and woodwork, or the British Museum Guides to the Department of British Antiquities, and you will appreciate their value.

(4) Similarly, the reports, transactions and other publications of learned and scientific societies usually consist of new material otherwise unpublished, yet much of this vast output only reaches a limited public. Some, undoubtedly, is highly specialized and restricted in its appeal, but it is better to go to a little trouble to sort out such items than to miss really useful material. Therefore, if you are a reasonably advanced worker in any field of inquiry, it behoves you to see what societies exist, and, if at all possible, at least scan regularly the contents of their publications. (See also Chapter Six.)

CHAPTER FIVE

GUIDES TO BOOKS

WE have now reached the stage when you have examined
without success all the likely books provided in the libraries
to which you have ready access.

The next step is to discover (a) whether any other likely
books exist, and (b) if so, where they are to be seen or how
you can obtain them, or (c) whether the information you
require is included in a publication which you have overlooked. You will, in other words, consider next (a) bibliographies, i.e. lists of, and guides to, books; (b) libraries, their
contents and facilities; and (c) guides to the *contents* of
books. Much of this ground has been summarized in the
author's HOW TO USE BOOKS, and since, as far as possible, the
information given there is not repeated, the reader is
advised to consult that companion volume.

Two brief warnings before we proceed: firstly, it must be
clear that the inquirer will not always, or even usually,
proceed in the order in which this survey is written. The
method of approach (see Chapter Eight) depends upon the
inquiry, and there are many short cuts.

Secondly, be sure that the facts when you find them will
be worth the trouble you are taking. Use discretion. Much
time can be expended in searching for a single elusive item
of information. Are you justified in spending that time?
You alone know. The 'I'm-not-going-to-be-beaten' feeling
and the 'detective' instinct are strong, so be on your guard.
There is, of course, no reason why, if you have nothing more
urgent to do, you should not pursue a quite useless inquiry
to the bitter end. Indeed, you will learn much in the process. At the same time remember that it is not fair to involve
others – library assistants or whoever they may be – in
frivolous inquiries. They will never ask you *why* you want

GUIDES TO BOOKS

their help; they take it for granted that the information
does matter. So don't abuse their good will.

We may now continue.

(*a*) What other likely books exist?

(1) First notice whether, in the books you have consulted, there are any references, either in the text, or in
lists (or bibliographies) at the end of the book or at the end
of chapters. Glance through these, looking for likely books.
Some of those mentioned may be in your library. Reference
may be made to data included in books on other subjects.
You may receive hints for further fields of inquiry.

(2) Find out what bibliographies there are in the library,
either general or specially relating to your field (see HOW
TO USE BOOKS).

Make full notes of the author, title, date, etc., of any books
you feel it would be useful to consult if that may be possible
(see later). Note briefly any particulars which will help you to
decide which of those you list should be *most* likely. Possibly,
when you have been through your bibliographies you will
have noted a dozen or more 'possibles'; you can't ask to
see them all at once; you must decide which to try first.

(3) And this is a step only to be taken if the inquiry is
important; the matter is included here only for completeness' sake – if the available bibliographies are not fruitful,
find out what *other* bibliographies exist. Important bibliographies are included in such standard lists as MINTO'S
REFERENCE BOOKS, MUDGE'S REFERENCE BOOKS, MCCOLVIN'S
LIBRARY STOCK, and the BRITISH MUSEUM LIST OF BOOKS
OF REFERENCE (see HOW TO USE BOOKS). Next – don't
be alarmed at the ensuing complication – you turn
to *bibliographies of bibliography*, guide-books to guidebooks. The most important of these is undoubtedly

T. BESTERMAN'S WORLD BIBLIOGRAPHY OF BIBLIO
GRAPHIES, 2 vols., 1939-40,

in which some 25,000 separately published bibliographies
are listed according to their subjects.

For later bibliographies – not only those in book form but

also bibliographies which appear as pamphlets, parts of other books or as periodical articles – see another of those fine 'tools' for which we are indebted to the American H. W. Wilson Co.,

THE BIBLIOGRAPHIC INDEX

published since 1937, with annual and five-yearly cumulations.

W. P. COURTNEY'S REGISTER OF NATIONAL BIBLIOGRAPHY,
3 vols., 1905-12,

an earlier, British, work is still useful.

C. S. NORTHUP'S REGISTER OF BIBLIOGRAPHIES OF THE
ENGLISH LANGUAGE AND LITERATURE, 1925,

is rather wider in scope than the title would imply.

(*b*) Is the information contained in part of a book more general in scope, or which, for some reason, you have overlooked?

Collections of essays or shorter papers might include one on your topic; there might even be an article in a periodical (see later). There are a few publications designed to help you to trace such shorter items which, otherwise, it is extremely difficult to discover. The two most useful works are both American, though they embrace a great deal of British material. The most up to date is the

ESSAY AND GENERAL LITERATURE INDEX, 1900-33,

an index to about 40,000 essays and articles in over 2000 volumes of collections and miscellaneous works, with annual supplements keeping it up to date (and a seven-year cumulation for 1934-40).

For earlier material see:

THE A.L.A. INDEX TO GENERAL LITERATURE, 1900,
WITH SUPPLEMENT, 1910.

This is a subject index to collections of essays and monographs, important parts and chapters of books, books which deal with several subjects, etc. It is out of date, but, on the other hand, most of the items included can be obtained fairly easily.

ALFRED COTGREAVE'S A CONTENTS-SUBJECT INDEX TO
GENERAL AND PERIODICAL LITERATURE, 1900,
is again useful only for older books.

There is also a fair amount of 'analysis' of book contents in some good library catalogues (e.g. those of the London Library), and probably in that of your own institution.

Periodicals – and remember that the heading embraces hundreds of most important technical, scientific and learned journals as well as more popular publications – are covered by

THE SUBJECT INDEX TO PERIODICALS,
published by the Library Association, which embraces the period from 1915, and is now issued annually; and by a series of American publications which began with

POOLE'S INDEX TO PERIODICAL LITERATURE
which, with supplements, covered the period from 1802 to 1906. This was followed by the

ANNUAL LIBRARY INDEX, 1905-10,
when the work was taken over by an already existing publication,

THE READER'S GUIDE TO PERIODICAL LITERATURE,
published by the H. W. Wilson Co., which now carries on the valuable work with monthly indexes (appearing quickly on the heels of the periodicals it covers and so being especially useful for current information), which are cumulated at quarterly and annual intervals to form larger and more convenient volumes.

THE READER'S GUIDE embraces those periodicals most generally taken by American libraries, but a companion publication indexes additional papers:

THE READER'S GUIDE SUPPLEMENT, later called

THE INTERNATIONAL INDEX TO PERIODICALS.

All the Wilson indexes also embrace some composite books.

The above-mentioned are general in scope. There are others limited to special subjects, among them THE AGRI-CULTURAL INDEX, THE INDUSTRIAL ARTS INDEX, THE EDUCA-

TION INDEX, and THE INDEX TO LEGAL PERIODICALS (Wilson publications), and THE DRAMATIC INDEX (published by Faxon). Useful English indexes are

> C. L. GOMME'S INDEX TO ARCHAEOLOGICAL PAPERS FROM 1665-1914,

since when the ground has been covered by the Library Association Index, and

> THE ROYAL SOCIETY OF LONDON, CATALOGUE OF SCIENTIFIC PAPERS, 1800-1900.

(c) If the book, or other likely source, is not in your local library, how can you obtain it?

This question is answered in HOW TO USE BOOKS, so it is only necessary to say here, firstly, that your library is probably in touch with the National Central Library in London, and can, with its aid, obtain on loan most of the books you may require, and secondly, that there are many fine non-public libraries – national, university, society, departmental, even private – at which the serious student is welcome and will be given every possible assistance.

There is little need for anyone to go without information if he will only use libraries fully and intelligently.

(d) When specific information is required it may not be necessary to obtain the book itself, or to go to some other library to see it. Probably your local librarian can get his colleague at the library where there is a copy to transcribe the required data (if it is brief) and send it by post.

Another facility, which is particularly useful where plans, drawings or tables are concerned, is occasionally available. A few large libraries (e.g. Birmingham Public Library) have a photostat installation and can provide exact photographic copies of the pages of books at a very reasonable cost.

It is not too much to say, in concluding this section of the book, that the book supply services, the library facilities of this country, are far in advance of the use made of them by the general public. They can be of much greater value than they are as yet to the student and inquirer, who do not at present take anything like the fullest advantage of the opportunities they offer. It is for such as read this book to remedy this position. Anyone who has ever engaged in publicity work knows how difficult it is to reach all who should be informed. Though a number of libraries have, rightly, endeavoured to 'advertise' their facilities, others have not done so, for lack of staff or funds, or because existing demands occupied their full attention. No one who reads this book should have any excuse for not getting all the books and information he needs; but it is hoped that each reader will go further and, by telling his friends of the opportunities libraries afford, help to make the library service better known and even more useful.

CHAPTER SIX

PERIODICALS AND OTHER SOURCES

THE fact-finder will soon discover that, saving in a few exceptional instances, the world of periodical literature is a difficult, tiresome and unsatisfactory one in which to search. We must read periodicals of many types, from the daily newspaper to technical journals and religious reviews, in order to keep informed regarding new ideas and recent events. But to turn to periodicals, seeking, perhaps, a single fact, is quite another matter, and unless that fact is obviously one which you will *not* find in books you are well advised to turn to periodicals only as a last resort. So many periodicals are diffuse and not arranged for convenience of reference; important items are buried in an often ill-assorted conglomeration of trivialities.

Nevertheless, there are exceptions and, moreover, there are *some* facts which you will find nowhere else.

(*a*) You need periodicals for the latest information.

Books are always to some extent out of date. Normally, it takes several months at least to write, print and publish a book. Anything which comes to light after the proofs are passed for the printer must be left out. Besides, new books on each topic are not issued every few weeks or even every few years, but only when there is sufficient new material or new ideas to justify new books – at least such *should* be the conditions.

For everything later than the latest book you must turn to periodicals, and (especially in such constantly changing spheres as science, technology, economics and politics) this latest data is probably of considerable importance.

(*b*) Much of the information in periodicals *never* finds its way into books. It may not be of sufficient general interest; it may be of purely temporary value or local appeal.

(*c*) From the periodicals of the past we can often learn better than from books (which are usually written some while after the events by men who see them in a different perspective) what the contemporary attitude was, how people reacted to conditions, how they viewed their own times. The student of social and political history may benefit by thus going back to contemporary records.

In view of the above, clearly, the inquirer will *have* to use periodicals frequently, so let us examine the position.

(1) The average library (excluding those in the bigger towns which do much more) takes a selection of from fifty to one hundred and fifty or more of those in most general demand, and current numbers may be seen in the reading rooms. The back numbers of purely ephemeral publications are kept for about three months, while the most valuable are permanently preserved. Nearly all libraries keep complete files of *The Times*, of local publications, and of such monthlies as *The Studio* and *The Connoisseur*. Otherwise the inquirer must apply to the larger libraries.

It is not, however, generally known that sets of some two hundred and fifty periodicals indexed in the Library Association's SUBJECT INDEX TO PERIODICALS may be borrowed through the inter-library loan scheme.

(2) Sets of back numbers can usually be seen, often free of charge, at the publishing office of each periodical. Back numbers can sometimes be purchased, though this might be a waste of money unless you are fairly certain the article will be useful. In urgent cases it *might* be worth trying to borrow the back numbers from the publishers (if there were not copies available for purchase), and in this event the publishers would be more likely to lend to a responsible body like a public library than to an individual inquirer.

(3) Make use of the indexes mentioned in the previous chapter. In addition, most periodicals which are of anything approaching permanent value (e.g. *The Engineer*, *The Studio*, *The Architect*) publish their own annual (or volume) indexes, which should be used.

(4) Lists of periodicals on different subjects are given in
HOW TO USE BOOKS. Other lists are

THE A.S.L.I.B. DIRECTORY (see Chapter Seven),

THE BRITISH MUSEUM CATALOGUE OF PERIODICAL PUBLI-
CATIONS,

THE PATENT OFFICE SUBJECT INDEX OF THE PERIODICAL
PUBLICATIONS,

THE WORLD LIST OF SCIENTIFIC PERIODICALS, 1900-21,
edited by A. W. Pollard and W. A. Smith.

THE UNION CATALOGUE OF THE PERIODICAL PUBLICATIONS
IN THE UNIVERSITY LIBRARIES OF THE BRITISH ISLES,
1937,

and

THE TIMES TERCENTENARY HAND LIST OF ENGLISH AND
WELSH NEWSPAPERS, MAGAZINES AND REVIEWS,
1920.

(5) For information on current events of all kinds, a file
of *The Times* is the most useful source, because (apart from
other reasons) alone of English newspapers (there is also an
index to *The Glasgow Herald*), it is provided with an official
index to all the items mentioned in its pages, commencing
in 1906 and continued quarterly.

Unofficial and much less complete is

PALMER'S INDEX TO THE TIMES,

but, as this was started as long ago as 1791, for the years
prior to 1906 it is essential.

(6) For tracing references to the events, etc., of the last
few days or weeks an extremely useful publication is

KEESING'S CONTEMPORARY ARCHIVES,

and may be seen at many libraries. It gives a digest of the
news of the world, with much useful information about
preceding events in their relation to current happenings, so
making the news of the day much more understandable
than is often done in the newspapers. New sheets, issued
every few days, are kept in loose-leaf files, and a unique
feature is the index, which is kept right up-to-date, a *new*
index for the whole year being, in fact, issued every week.

As the Index to *The Times* is always a little out-of-date, being issued only at quarterly intervals, KEESING'S CONTEMPORARY ARCHIVES is valuable if only as a supplement; actually, the concise data is most satisfactory, and in every respect the publication deserves well of students of current affairs, and merits the increased support of public libraries.

(7) When consulting files of periodicals, especially newspapers, remember that they are mostly made up according to plan. That is to say, the various features and types of news, as a rule, appear day by day, week by week, on much the same pages – it may be, foreign news on the page before the centre, court and official intelligence on the page after the centre, sport at the back, finance at the front after the advertisements, and so on. If you are searching for an item of news of which you do not know the date, notice where such news are *usually* given and look on that page only in the first instance. Try elsewhere only if the method fails.

(8) Many papers make a feature of 'Answers to Correspondents', thereby rendering their readers a most useful service. When you cannot find the facts required in books, and if the query is of a suitable type, you are well advised to make use of this aid. Do not, however, tender your difficulties to the editor of the local *Argus* or *Courier* (unless they are 'local' matters). Select a paper which specializes in the subject. Study the periodicals; some are useless, as you will soon see by examining the 'Answers' column or noting its absence, while others are excellent. For example, *The Artist* makes a speciality of inquiries from art students, and *John o'London's Weekly* of literary questions. The 'Answers to Correspondents' column is a strong feature in many gardening and technical periodicals.

There is one paper,

NOTES AND QUERIES,

which exists solely as a medium for the asking and answering of questions. Its readers are chiefly interested in literary, historical, archaeological and genealogical matters, but in one sense there is no limit to its scope.

Some papers (e.g. the *Daily Telegraph* and *The Times Literary Supplement*) will occasionally even print letters asking for information if they are of sufficient general interest.

One cannot leave the subject of newspapers, especially when the word is related to information, without a few words of warning. An absolutely impartial man has never existed, for it is impossible not to have feelings, sentiments, views and ideals; consequently, it is too much to expect any newspaper, since it is made by men, to be impartial. All one may ask is a fair, adequate and reasonably complete presentation of affairs. Unfortunately, however, the newspaper of to-day can exercise such a powerful influence upon public opinion that we cannot wonder that it is so often used, not to present the unadulterated facts, but to influence the unthinking masses in directions advantageous to the proprietors or to the interests with which they are associated. Furthermore, since newspapers are, first and foremost, commercial undertakings, and since the vast majority of readers ask for nothing better than sensation, scandal, scares and stunts, is it not natural if some newspapers do their best to provide them?

There are a few newspapers which, preferring to appeal to the intelligent minority, remain true to the ideals of journalism. They have their policies and politics, for without them they would lack vitality, but they try to be honest. Such are the *Manchester Guardian*, the *Daily Telegraph*, *The Times*, the *Sunday Times* and *The Observer* – *not* an exhaustive list. There are, however, others which need not be specified, which, when they are not sensational, are superficial. They seize upon the trivial; they exaggerate; they actually lie, not perhaps by publishing any item of news which is not strictly true, but by a skilful process of eliminating some aspects and expanding others, of publishing news without stating its source, by leading readers to suppose that news is official and definite when it is really based upon irresponsible gossip. Such methods are far more pernicious than actual falsehood; a lie can be detected, but a misrepresentation of the full truth is only too readily accepted as a true statement.

The reader must decide whether to leave all suspect journals severely alone or to read them with a full realization of their failings. When looking for information they are best left alone. Always exercise discretion if the subject is one liable to journalistic colouring.

Before any fact or item of news featured in a popular newspaper is treated as an item of information it should be checked by reference to one of the better-class papers. If this is done for a period it is easy to acquire a sense of discrimination as to the sources of news, which will prevent one being misled. The sensational double-column heading of the popular paper is often based on a brief telegram of doubtful authenticity. Unfortunately, denials of false news are very seldom published.

Apart from books and periodicals there are many types of printed material, maps and illustrations in which information may be found. Neither preserved nor utilized as much as they should be – because, for one thing, it is troublesome to store, arrange and consult such single detached items – in case of need the inquirer should not overlook them.

The technical and commercial departments of the large libraries collect and systematically exploit this miscellany; nearly all public libraries preserve it when it has any connection with the locality.

Here one can only give notes on a few aspects.

(1) Maps and plans may serve many purposes in addition to the obvious one of showing the relative location of places. The practised hand can, indeed, get a very good idea of what a place *looks* like by studying a map. He can tell, for example, which districts are probably dull and which beautiful, can discover whether a stretch of coastline is flat and sandy or whether there are cliffs. By means of character-

istic signs numerous features of interest, such as buildings
of archaeological significance, lighthouses, windmills, inns
and churches are indicated.

Especially to be noted – because so easily overlooked – are
those maps (and atlases) which are designed to convey, not
topographical features, but other information – climate
(winds, rainfall), types of vegetation, geological formation,
economic products, historical development and the like.
Maps of this character are included in many general atlases.

A few useful special atlases are:

PHILIP'S HISTORICAL ATLAS,

POOLE'S HISTORICAL ATLAS OF MODERN EUROPE,

SHEPHERD'S HISTORICAL ATLAS,

MACMILLAN'S HISTORICAL ATLAS OF THE BRITISH EMPIRE,

BARTHOLOMEW'S LITERARY AND HISTORICAL ATLAS
(4 vols. in Everyman's Library),

BARTHOLOMEW'S PHYSICAL ATLAS,

THE OXFORD ECONOMIC ATLAS,

PHILIP'S MERCANTILE MARINE ATLAS,

and

PHILIP'S CHAMBER OF COMMERCE ATLAS.

Good general atlases are:

PHILIP'S NEW COMMERCIAL, INTERNATIONAL and NEW
HANDY GENERAL ATLASES,

PHILIP'S RECORD ATLAS,

THE TIMES SURVEY ATLAS OF THE WORLD,

BARTHOLOMEW'S CITIZEN'S ATLAS,

and

STANFORD'S LONDON ATLAS OF UNIVERSAL GEOGRAPHY.

We must admit, however, that there are not any really
up-to-date large atlases. Map making is an expensive branch
of publishing, and wars and upheavals and the alteration of
place names to meet changing national and racial ideas have
not made the cartographer's task an easy one. Nevertheless the well-known firms, such as Philip, Bartholomew,
Stanford, Geographia, etc., do endeavour to meet special

current requirements and so, if you have any particular needs, you are well advised to write to them or visit their offices.

Odham's recent NEW ILLUSTRATED ATLAS, though small and inexpensive attempts to portray the post-war world; and for maps on matter of current interest consult SERIAL MAPS, published monthly.

When buying an atlas for home use get the largest and best you can afford, because, though it is true of most books that the bigger they are the more information they contain, this is especially the case with atlases. The more different maps, the larger the scale, the more of the less important places, which are just those which you will have need to trace, can it embrace.

Of single-sheet maps there are thousands for different purposes and of varying value. For Great Britain you cannot possibly better the ORDNANCE SURVEY sheets – of which the 'one-inch to the mile' are fully adequate for all but the most detailed purposes. For motoring, the half-inch or quarter-inch sheets are preferable. See, however, the National Book League's Book Lists, 'Maps' and 'Atlases'.

(2) Collections of prints, photographs and pictures of all kinds are frequently made by public libraries. Most have local collections, ranging from a few engravings to elaborate regional surveys, comprising copies of most of the existing prints, photographs of practically every place and building (however slight its interest), portraits of all notable residents, records of local events, of popular customs, costume, archaeological finds and natural history. Although the inquirer's interest might not be in the locality, cross-sections of these local collections may be extremely valuable. For example, if you need a portrait of anyone, apply to the local collection at the town where he was born; or, again, students of Roman antiquities, or birds, or folklore, will find these local records, though naturally limited in scope, useful contributions to the material.

Some other libraries have general illustration collections,

intended for the use of schools, artists and the general public. The value of these collections is twofold. In the first place the items are closely classified, so that it is often much easier to find a picture of any place, person, thing or event than it would be to search in books. Secondly, much pictorial material is preserved which would otherwise be destroyed – portraits, photographs of recent happenings and discoveries culled from the illustrated weeklies, plates from discarded books, and so on.

(3) Art galleries and museums will often include question-answering items (see also Chapter Seven).

(4) Trade catalogues and price lists, because of the descriptions, specifications and illustrations they contain, embrace data unobtainable elsewhere. A few of the larger libraries make collections of up-to-date catalogues. In certain instances the manufacturers will send them to you on request.

(5) Some people have a horror of *time-tables* and much exaggerate their complexity. Actually, any person of average intelligence who will take care should not find the slightest difficulty, or ever make such mistakes as will cause him to wait in the early hours of the morning for a train that doesn't leave until after lunch. Always look at all the notes, indicated, as a rule, by letters against the times or at the head or foot of the column; notice carefully how times before midday and times after midday are indicated, remembering that, for instance, 1 a.m. is in the middle of the night and not lunch time; use the index and turn up all references, as the town may be served by more than one line, in which case you must compare the services; if a cross-country journey is to be made, look for possible through services.

The best comprehensive British time-table is BRAD-SHAW'S; for Londoners the A B C TIME-TABLE is much the handiest; while the time-tables of all the companies may be had for a few coppers. Always be sure you are using a *current* time-table.

If you suffer from an inferiority complex where time-tables are concerned, ask someone to give you a few minutes' instruction – perhaps the assistant at your library some time when he is not busy with other readers. We used to play a Bradshaw game. The referee selected two, usually widely separated, places, and the winner was he who first discovered the best route and train from one to the other. It is not bad fun, if marooned on a wet day, to practise working out imaginary journeys, and the skill acquired may be useful in the future.

CHAPTER SEVEN

PERSONAL INQUIRIES

FINALLY, should the sources already discussed be fruitless, a personal inquiry in the right quarter will often bring the required information.

There are many organizations – official and non-official – whose chief function it is to collect and provide information. There are other societies and institutions which, while primarily intended to further the particular interests of their members, will willingly extend whatever help is reasonable to the general inquirer. There are even individuals who, in certain circumstances, are ready to put their private collections and personal experience at your disposal.

Perhaps because these helpers are not sufficiently known, perhaps because the ordinary man hesitates to approach them, they are not utilized as often as they might be.

Remember, however, what has been said already about private information. There *are* things which you cannot expect to be told – facts which the owners reserve for their own advantage or which are not for general circulation. Inquiries of this type will be futile, and may be impertinent.

Another type of inquiry to be strictly avoided is that which belongs to the rightful province of any profession or occupation, or which seeks information which you could obtain in the normal way on payment of usual fees and charges from a professional man. You must not expect people to give away the knowledge they have to sell for a living. Don't, for example, try to solve a practical legal, or medical, or architectural problem by inquiry; you must obviously employ a solicitor, or doctor, or architect in the ordinary way. But, on the other hand, it is possible that a lawyer would willingly give you information on the *history* of law if, say, you wished to settle a point arising in historical studies (it all depends upon circumstances, of course), or a medical society provide data of a non-professional character to be applied to some recognized voluntary social purpose. And so on. Personal inquiry must be conducted with discretion, but that does not mean that, *when justified*, it should not be made.

The words 'when justified' are italicized, because it is only right that, whenever you propose to cause trouble to any organization or person, you should be certain that you really want the information, and that it will benefit yourself or others. It would be a great disservice to all concerned if the writer advocated personal inquiry and mentioned sources without also emphasizing this point. Never make a frivolous inquiry; never make any personal inquiry until you have exhausted all other possible sources; never do so unless it is genuinely important.

Often you will not be asked for any payment. If, however, your inquiry involves research or expense, or occupies more than a few minutes of your helper's time, you should be willing to pay reasonable fees. There is no need, however, to hesitate to make the preliminary inquiry lest you involve yourself in expense. You will usually be informed if any charge is to be made before the work is put in hand, and if you have any doubts you can make the point quite clear by asking to be informed before any expenses are incurred.

To whom, then, may you turn for personal assistance?

(a) *The Staffs of Libraries.* Probably sufficient has been said to show the reader that the library in his town is the natural clearing-house for information. Quite apart from the books it contains, it usually endeavours to provide an *information* service also. Undoubtedly, before many years there will be a national information service similar to the existing national book service, and when that time comes the local library will be the inquirer's key to the information resources of the whole country. Even now, the public library can *get* information often much better and more

77

easily than any private individual. It is in touch with other organizations; it can make an impersonal approach; it has better 'standing' than the private person in many instances. Therefore, take your inquiries to your library unless experience has shown that this is not worth while. Libraries vary considerably in their interest in reference work and in their facilities for conducting it. There are a few libraries known to the writer which make it a point of honour *never* to tell an inquirer that they cannot help him until they have exhausted every possible channel of inquiry. Other libraries, probably because they have not the staff or funds, will not go beyond an examination of their own resources.

Don't, of course, expect the library to take all the work off your shoulders. If research through books, periodicals, etc., is involved, it is sufficient if the staff puts the material at your disposal, shows you all the likely places to look, and then leaves you to do the actual searching yourself. Usually they will themselves find the answers to simple questions, or to those requiring special knowledge of sources, but you must not, for example, expect them to go through parish registers to trace your ancestors, or to make extracts, or do anything, in fact, which, given the material, you can do yourself.

A majority of libraries have special collections and the presence of a special collection generally means that the services of some member of the staff particularly qualified in that subject are available. For example, there is a fine library and museum, devoted to the poet Keats and his circle, at the Heath Branch of the Hampstead Public Library, and the librarian-in-charge there has a very extensive knowledge of every aspect of Keats's life, work, critics, friends, etc.

Similarly – and these are but examples – the librarians in charge of the fine music collections at Manchester, Liverpool and Edinburgh Public Libraries and of the great Shakespeare collection at Birmingham Public Library have a very wide and expert knowledge of their respective fields.

Particulars of special collections will be found in the A.S.L.I.B. DIRECTORY (see later) and in the

LIBRARIES, MUSEUMS AND ART GALLERIES YEAR BOOK, published by A. J. Philip of Gravesend and of which the latest edition appeared in 1937.

See also RYE'S GUIDE TO THE LIBRARIES OF LONDON.

Nearly all libraries have good local collections, covering every aspect of the history, topography, antiquities, natural history, etc., of the town and country. For 'local' information the best place to try is, undoubtedly, the chief library in the area concerned.

Particularly valuable are the library's facilities for business men, manufacturers and the like. Some of the larger industrial centres (such as Manchester, Leeds, Liverpool, Birmingham, Bristol, Hull and Sheffield) have large and important Commercial and Technical Departments, in which the latest available data is arranged minutely to facilitate reference. Though primarily intended for the use of local firms and residents, suitable inquiries by post or telephone from those living elsewhere will seldom, if ever, be refused attention.

(b) *The Staffs of Museums.* The man in the street is apt to look upon museums as places where fascinating and beautiful things of all kinds are stored and displayed for the mildly educational enjoyment of sightseers. This is far from being their principal function. The real value of museums lies in the fact that they collect, arrange, and make available, scientific, artistic and historical information, being particularly concerned with those aspects of knowledge where it is necessary or valuable to be able to see, and perhaps handle, the actual objects involved. They collect specimens, not for the sake of collecting, but because those specimens give information.

They are in charge of curators, who in addition to a good general knowledge of the field covered by their collections, are generally specialists in one or other branch. Their services are always at the disposal of *bona-fide* inquirers, and usually they take a broad view of their educational duties.

The extent and nature of the assistance you may obtain will obviously depend upon the size and scope of the museum, which may be anything from a little inferior gathering of oddments to the marvellous national collections at South Kensington and Bloomsbury. Even the smaller ones can often answer queries relating to local matters and to reasonably common scientific, archaeological and artistic objects. At the larger institutions (and the smaller specialized ones) the inquirer can secure, freely, the help and advice of some of the greatest living expert authorities.

Inquiries can be made by post or personally. If your query concerns an object of any kind, be it a butterfly or a fossil, if at all possible take or send the actual specimen in the first instance, as you will find it impossible to describe most things with sufficient accuracy to serve.

The best list of museums of all types is the

DIRECTORY OF MUSEUMS AND ART GALLERIES IN THE
BRITISH ISLES,

published by the Museums Association in 1931, and giving full particulars of their scope, special features, educational activities and publications. A number are mentioned in the A.S.L.I.B. DIRECTORY, and in the LIBRARIES, MUSEUMS AND ART GALLERIES YEAR BOOK which gives a closely packed 25-page 'Subject Index to Special Collections' in libraries and museums.

(c) *Official Departments and Institutions.* Since it is the duty of governments to promote the public well-being in every possible way, not the least important of their activities, though probably the least generally known, are those concerned with the collection and dissemination of information. Considerable sums of money (though probably nothing like enough) are spent in this and other countries, and large staffs are employed with the express purpose of helping those engaged in commerce, industry, social welfare and other activities.

If your query is related to the work of any Government

department – and, of course, if it is a reasonable and important one – always approach the appropriate office.

For information of almost any kind relating to any colony, or to any foreign country, apply to the representatives in London of that nation, who will invariably give all possible help.

Much information can also be obtained at the London offices of colonial and foreign railways.

(d) *Newspaper Bureaux and Banks*. At the offices of some newspapers and periodicals – local, national, technical, economic and financial – up-to-date information bureaux are maintained, sometimes available to the general public, sometimes restricted to subscribers. The big banks also have information services for the benefit of their clients.

(e) *Societies and Institutions*. In Kelly's London Directory nineteen pages are devoted to the names and addresses of some three thousand societies, associations, institutions and the like, and probably this imposing list is far from complete, though it only covers the metropolis. Practically every field of activity is embraced, for whatever our interests may be, we find it highly desirable to keep in contact with those similarly engaged, in order to further our mutual aims, to exchange views and facilitate research. All these societies are to some extent clearing-houses for information, and there are few lines of inquiry in which help cannot be obtained from one or other of these organizations.

Naturally they are of widely differing types – ranging from propagandist bodies which will be only too willing to provide information (even though, possibly, the inquirer might need to allow for propagandist bias) to these professional and commercial groups which exist for the exclusive benefit of their members, and to which inquiry would probably be useless.

The point, however, is that a society is an organization of people specially informed on their particular subject, and maybe making a feature of collecting and disseminating information. Obviously, it is very likely to be able to help the inquirer, though the extent will naturally depend upon the various circumstances.

The most valuable to the general reader are the (not exclusively-professional) learned, scientific, literary and artistic organizations. As a rule they are very willing to help, are courteous and interested. One cannot, for example, imagine a 'Dickens' or a 'Shakespeare' society, or an association of archaeologists, refusing to answer any question which did not involve research or private information. It goes without saying that if the inquirer is specially interested in the matter, if he is likely to have frequent need of the society's help, and if laymen are admitted, he would probably find it to his advantage to join; on the other hand, the inquiries of non-members are not usually ignored. The truth of the matter is that there is much more goodwill and helpfulness in this world – and especially in the world of learning and art – than is generally recognized. Many of us go without the help of those who might be delighted to serve people with kindred interests because we are timid and reluctant. Ask yourself whether you would refuse to supply, even to a stranger, any specialized information you might possess. You would not, one is sure, unless it was definitely contrary to your personal or professional interests, or unless it involved appreciable time and trouble.

Even professional, technical and similar bodies will often give advice and information which is not of a purely technical and professional character.

Inquiries should be by letter addressed to the secretary.

A detailed list, giving particulars of membership, publications, activities, etc., is to be found in

THE OFFICIAL YEAR BOOK OF THE SCIENTIFIC AND LEARNED SOCIETIES OF GREAT BRITAIN AND IRELAND, which embraces organizations devoted to science generally, astronomy, mathematics and physics, chemistry and photography, geography, geology and mineralogy, biology, microscopy and anthropology, economic sciences and statistics, mechanical sciences and architecture, naval and military science, agriculture and horticulture, law, literature, history and music, psychology, archaeology and medicine.

A thirty-page list is included in WHITAKER'S ALMANACK, while a valuable classified survey appears in the A.S.L.I.B. DIRECTORY.

(*f*) *Trade Associations, etc., and Firms.* Subject again to the reservation that data definitely exclusive to the trade or firm cannot be supplied to any outsider, trade and commercial associations (and even individual business concerns) will often answer suitable inquiries. Some of the former have, indeed, a certain publicity function when, clearly, the answering of personal inquiries is a legitimate part of their activity, while, to put the matter at its lowest level, the alert business undertaking knows that by helping the inquirer it is at least creating goodwill.

(*g*) Finally, there are even *private individuals* willing to place their personal collections and resources at the disposal of *bona-fide* research workers.

It will be seen that there *are* plenty of potential helpers. At the same time, the writer realizes that the foregoing paragraphs are valuable only if the inquirer can discover particular examples of societies, etc., to help *him*. That is not always an easy task, but it is made much easier by the existence of a comprehensive survey of sources, including hundreds of specific examples of all the types mentioned above.

To this book the writer would direct the special attention of all readers. It is

THE A.S.L.I.B. DIRECTORY,

a guide to sources of specialized information in Great Britain and Ireland, published in 1928 by the Association of Special Libraries and Information Bureaux, with the assistance of the Carnegie United Kingdom Trust. Copies may be seen at most libraries.

Undoubtedly it is the most important single contribution yet made towards establishing a national information service. It is primarily an analysis of the contents of specialist libraries, designed to show the student where he can obtain books on his particular subject. The scope of the Directory, however, is very much wider. First of all it includes not only books, but many other types of material – photographs, maps, newspaper cuttings, etc. Secondly, it gives particulars of hundreds of information bureaux, established by institutions, societies, firms, etc. Thirdly, it lists the most useful periodicals on each subject. In brief, it is a classified guide to all the important places where books and information are to be found, telling the resources and limitations of each, and to whom and on what conditions help can be given.

As there are over three hundred large, double-column pages of subject entries (followed by a full directory), the best way to indicate the wide range it covers will be to quote some of the subject headings, opening the book at random: marriage and divorce, Captain Marryat, Karl Marx, Mary Queen of Scots, massage and medical gymnastics, matches and match-boxes, materia medica, maternity and child welfare, mathematical instruments, mathematics, Mazarinades, mechanical engineering, medals, medical missions, medicine and surgery, menageries, mental disease and therapy, menus, mercantile law, mercantile marine, mesmerism, Methodists, metric system, Mexico, mezzo-tints, and so on. Clearly this is a book to help *every* inquirer.

Unfortunately it is somewhat out of date, but it should be remembered that though collections established since 1928 are naturally not mentioned most of those which were then listed are still functioning. Moreover, up-to-date information is available at the offices of A.S.L.I.B.

May we remind you also of the information service provided to members of the NATIONAL BOOK LEAGUE (described in HOW TO USE BOOKS).

CHAPTER EIGHT

MORE ABOUT METHOD

VERY little space remains. It would be easy to fill many more pages with descriptive lists of sources. But as 'method' is no less essential than 'material', in this last short chapter let us briefly review and amplify our remarks on the former aspect.

There is no standard method which should be used in every instance; each inquiry is different in its nature, purpose and difficulty, and must be handled individually. If time were no consideration we could work according to a regulation plan, proceeding step by step until we succeeded. But time *is* a consideration, always. It is not enough to be thorough; we must be quick, too. Therefore, though the inquirer should know all the possible stages in a thorough inquiry programme, he must take short cuts, deciding at which stage it is best to commence, endeavouring to omit as many steps as possible.

Experience and knowledge are the best time-savers.

You cannot know too much about sources of information, both general and special. They deserve careful examination. Some part of whatever time you devote to the study of your subjects should be set aside for the systematic consideration of reference books, periodicals, indexes and the like. You will gradually accumulate considerable time-saving power. If you know only *one* good reference book – what it contains and what it doesn't, how to abstract facts from it quickly and accurately – you have acquired a useful asset.

Our first rule is 'try the most likely places first'. How are you to know what places are 'likely' if you have no knowledge of any sources?

There is also much to be done, mentally, before you go to sources at all.

First of all, define your inquiry. What exactly is it that you want to know? State the precise fact. Narrow it down, shedding all the unessentials. Analyse it; it may be a composite query, embracing two or more facts which may or may not be found together.

Next, classify it. Ask yourself to what subject or branch of knowledge it belongs.

Does it relate to a person, a place, an event, a saying? If so, certain types of reference books will be suggested.

Is it of such a nature that some special form of fact-presentation is indicated? e.g. is it likely to be found in 'official' or 'society' publications, or in statistical works?

Are there any obvious limitations – national, or time? The date of the information is an important limiting factor. If the facts must be up to date, if the event is recent, all but the latest books of all kinds must be eliminated; recourse to periodicals or annuals may be clearly indicated. Or, on the contrary, the fact may relate to a past time or an obsolete process, when research in older sources may obviously be best at first.

If you have to refer to an index, or to a dictionary, or encyclopaedia, ask yourself under what word it will be mentioned. Think of synonymous terms and alternatives. If you have to turn to a systematic work, glance through the list of contents to decide which chapter is most appropriate.

Very few queries can belong to one branch of knowledge, to one type of treatment and one only. Remember that all things in this world are closely interrelated and interwoven. Sciences are applied in industry; history may be made up of the achievements of individuals; the practical is based on theory, and the theoretical can be illustrated by practice.

Ask yourself to what provinces of knowledge your question may belong. Write it down fully and clearly and examine each word in detail. Let us, to illustrate this point, suppose you seek information on the following:

(a) The coat of arms and motto of the Blank family.

Three subjects — coats of arms (heraldry), mottoes (perhaps books of quotations), the Blank family. The last may be dealt with in a family history or in the lives of individual members. Even then you have not finished. Family history is often dealt with fully in county and local histories. What about portraits? — for old engravings often carry the arms.

(b) The production of wood pulp in Sweden.

Sweden. Wood pulp. Sweden treated generally. Sweden treated economically (with regard to productions). Statistics. World trade. Wood pulp is used for papermaking — books on paper, paper trade, etc.

(c) The house where the poet X was born. Two subjects. The life of the poet. Where is the house? Local history, topography, guide-books, etc. Illustrations, collections. Books on the homes and haunts of the poets, etc.

Most questions, when analysed, are found to have more than one association.

Having noted possible relations, select the most likely for examination first, but do not follow one branch to the bitter end. Proceed on one line of inquiry only through the most accessible sources; then do the same for the others; only if this fails pass on to less handy sources.

Keep these different lines in mind all the while, and if you have to handle any book in which more than one line may be covered, exhaust that book before passing on. For example, if you are looking for information about that poet's house and go to a general encyclopaedia, try under both the poet and the place on the same occasion. Avoid handling books, or visiting libraries, or writing to people, more than once for the same inquiry.

Remember where you have looked. If your inquiry is at all lengthy it is very easy to forget that you have already tried this book or that, and to waste time consulting it again. System will obviate this, but if there is any risk make a rough note of the books as you use them.

Be on the look out for clues. Books which don't satisfy

will often, nevertheless, suggest other books and other relationships.

Use your imagination. Think all the while of new possibilities and make a note of them.

Finally, when you *do* find the facts for which you are searching, weigh the evidence carefully. Be quite sure that what you find is what you have been looking for. It is quite easy, after a long and tiring search, to accept as 'good enough' information which is not really satisfactory. More than that, examine the facts. Everything that is printed is not, alas, correct, complete and up to date. Ask yourself if the book or other source is generally reliable, up to date, authoritative. If 'opinions', as distinct from 'facts', are involved, has the writer any bias? If so, how can it be corrected? If you have any doubts about the accuracy of a source, check it up by seeing how it deals with some matter about which you have personal knowledge or about which you can obtain independent reliable data. Don't fall into the trap of presuming that, because the facts are not what you had expected or wanted them to be, they are necessarily wrong. Don't ever imagine that from a comparison of two 'sides' of a case you will necessarily get the truth.

In short, always keep an open mind, allow for the personal equation, whether it operates in yourself or in your sources, be intelligent and bring as much knowledge and imagination as possible to bear upon your inquiries.

LIBRARIES: THEIR HISTORY AND USE

A short book list compiled by D. C. Henrik Jones, Librarian and Information Officer of the Library Association

HISTORY AND DESCRIPTION OF LIBRARIES

BARWICK, GEORGE FREDERICK. *The Reading Room of the British Museum.* (Benn) 1929. A chronicle showing the various changes from a small basement room to the present rotunda.

BOSTWICK, ARTHUR E. (Editor). *Popular Libraries of the World.* (American Library Association, Chicago; Woolston Book Co., Nottingham) 1933. Reports of the development of the popular library movement in 45 countries.

BOULTON, WILLIAM HENRY. *The Romance of the British Museum: The Story of its Origins, Growth and Purpose, and Some of its Contents.* (Low, Marston) 1931.

BUTLER, PIERCE (Editor). *Books and Libraries in Wartime.* (University of Chicago Press, Chicago; Cambridge University Press, London) 1945. 8s. 6d. Eight lectures in which attention is not only paid to the impact of war upon books and libraries, but also upon newspapers, moving pictures and radio.

CLARK, J. W. *The Care of Books: An Essay on the Development of Libraries and their Fittings from the Earliest Time to the End of the 18th Century.* (Cambridge University Press) 1909. A standard book on early library history.

EDWARDS, EDWARD. *Free Town Libraries: Their Formation, Management and History in Britain, France,*

Germany and America. (Trübner) 1869. The early history of public libraries. English and American are treated in detail; other countries more briefly; *Libraries and Founders of Libraries.* (Tr\u{u}bner) 1864. An historical survey of libraries, including ancient libraries, libraries of monasteries, libraries of famous authors and other personages abroad, and important English private libraries; *Lives of the Founders of the British Museum.* (Trübner) 1870. This includes notices of the chief benefactors, 1570-1870; *Memoirs of Libraries.* (Trubner) 1859. 2 vols. A very full general history; also describes most of the important classification schemes to 1850, and gives information on the compilation and printing of the British Museum catalogue.

ESDAILE, ARUNDELL. *The British Museum Library.* (Allen & Unwin) 1946; (Editor) *The World's Great Libraries.* (Grafton) 1934-1937; vol. I *National Libraries* by Arundell Esdaile; vol. II *Famous Libraries* by M. Burton. The history and chief contents of 31 national and 34 other great libraries.

KENYON, FREDERIC G. *Libraries and Museums.* (Benn) 1930. A brief general history, including an account of the origin and development of British public libraries.

MACRAY, WILLIAM DUNN. *Annals of the Bodleian Library, Oxford: With a Notice of the Earlier Library of the University.* (Oxford University Press) 1890. A standard history of the Library. An appendix contains lists of the MSS. and notes of special collections.

MINTO, JOHN. *A History of the Public Library Movement in Great Britain and Ireland.* (Allen & Unwin) 1932.

MUNTHE, WILHELM. *American Librarianship from a European Angle.* (American Library Association, Chicago; Woolston Book Co., Nottingham) 1939. A readable report on, and evaluation of, American policies and practice, by the Director of Oslo University Library.

NEWCOMBE, LUXMOORE. *The University and College Libraries of Great Britain and Ireland.* (Bumpus) 1927. A guide to 310 libraries for the research student with indexes of special collections and subjects.

RYE, REGINALD A. *The Students' Guide to the Libraries of London.* (University of London Press) 1927. Information about a great number of London libraries of all kinds, with descriptions of the most important collections, and historical notes.

SAVAGE, ERNEST A. *Old English Libraries.* (Methuen) 1911. The making, collection and use of books during the Middle Ages.

STREETER, BURNETT H. *The Chained Library: A Survey of Four Centuries in the Evolution of the English Library.* (Macmillan) 1931. This should be read in conjunction with Clark's *The Care of Books,* listed above. Further research into library development and fittings.

THOMPSON, J. W. *The Medieval Library.* (University of Chicago Press, Chicago; Cambridge University Press, London) 1939. A well-documented and detailed history covering mediaeval libraries in Europe and the Near East.

THORNTON, JOHN L. *The Chronology of Librarianship.* (Grafton) 1941. An introduction to the history of libraries and book-collecting from 4000 B.C.

WILSON, LOUIS R. *The Geography of Reading: A Study of the Distribution and Status of Libraries in the United States.* (University of Chicago Press, Chicago; Cambridge University Press, London) 1938. 22s. 6d. This work displays the striking variations of library service and other facilities for education and communication found in the various regions and states, and examines the causes contributing to these variations.

THE USE OF LIBRARIES

BAKER, ERNEST A. (Editor). *The Uses of Libraries*. (University of London Press) 1930. Information about the chief libraries of the world, especially British libraries, and how to use them.

BURTON, MARGARET, and VOSBURGH, MARION E. *A Bibliography of Librarianship: A Classified and Annotated Guide to the Library Literature of the World (Excluding Slavonic and Oriental Languages)*. (Library Association) 1934. 15s.

COWLEY, JOHN D. *The Use of Reference Material*. (Grafton) 1937. This describes essential reference works, and outlines their scope.

FLEXNER, JENNIE M. *Making Books Work: A Guide to the Use of Libraries*. (Simon & Schuster, New York) 1943. The library and its contents described in non-technical terms for the general and special reader.

HAYGOOD, WILLIAM CONVERSE. *Who Uses the Public Library?* (University of Chicago Press, Chicago; Cambridge University Press, London) 1938. 10s. 6d. An interpretation for the general public of facts about typical readers of the New York Public Library.

McCOLVIN, LIONEL R., and McCOLVIN, ERIC R. *Library Stock and Assistance to Readers*. (Grafton) 1936. Largely a textbook, but it may be read with profit by the general reader needing an introduction to the use of books.

SAVAGE, ERNEST A. *Special Librarianship in General Libraries and Other Papers*. (Grafton) 1939. Seven papers, or essays, on various aspects of 'special librarianship', others on aid to readers, book selection, professional training, and two excursions into historical bibliography.

THE PUBLIC LIBRARY SERVICE

BAKER, ERNEST A. *The Public Library*. (Grafton) 1924. A brief history of the public library movement and an account of the service given.

BOARD OF EDUCATION: DEPARTMENTAL COMMITTEE ON PUBLIC LIBRARIES. *Report*. (Kenyon Report) (H.M. Stationery Office) 1927. Reports on the position of public libraries up to 1927 with 139 pages of statistics. Among other matters, the National Central Library and library co-operation are the subject of important recommendations.

CARNELL, E. J. *County Libraries: Retrospect and Forecast*. (Grafton) 1938. A history of the county library movement, dealing also with the problems and ideals.

CARNOVSKY, LEON, and MARTIN, LOWELL (Editors). *The Library in the Community: Papers Presented Before the Library Institute at the University of Chicago, Aug. 23-28, 1943*. (University of Chicago Press, Chicago; Cambridge University Press, London) 1944. 14s. A description of the service given in varying communities, and consideration of how the community may affect the nature of the services the library provides.

INSTITUT INTERNATIONAL DE CO-OPERATION INTELLECTUELLE. *Bibliothèques Populaires et Loisirs Ouvriers*. (Institut International de Co-operation Intellectuelle, Paris) 1933. A description of the 'popular', or public, library movement in general, containing special studies on developments in different countries, mainly European.

JAST, L. STANLEY. *The Library and the Community*. (Nelson) 1939. A guide for the general reader stating what the public library is and what it stands for.

JOECKEL, CARLETON BRUNS, and CARNOVSKY, LEON. *A Metropolitan Library in Action: A Survey of the Chicago Public Library*. (University of Chicago Press,

Chicago; Cambridge University Press, London) 1940.
16s.6d. A comprehensive study of the administration and
activities of one of the largest public libraries in America.

LEYLAND, ERIC. *The Public Library and the Adolescent*.
(Grafton) 1935. The adolescent is here considered as a
separate class of borrower deserving special provision.

McCOLVIN, LIONEL R. *Libraries and the Public*. (Allen &
Unwin) 1937. 5s. A description for the general reader
of what the public library can and should provide; *The
Public Library System of Great Britain: A Report on
its Present Conditions with Proposals for Post-War
Re-organisation*. (Library Association) 1942.

WELLARD, J. H. *The Public Library Comes of Age*.
(Grafton) 1940. A discussion of the public library as a
social force and the relationship which should exist
between the library and the public.

SPECIAL KINDS OF LIBRARIES

JONES, E. K. *Hospital Libraries*. (American Library
Association, Chicago; Woolston Book Co., Nottingham)
1939. Hospital library organization, with special
attention paid to book selection for patients.

McCOLVIN, LIONEL R., and REEVES, H. *Music Libraries*.
(Grafton) 1937-1938. 2 vols. Vol. I deals with the
administration of music libraries, and vol. II contains
a classified list of music, a section on collections and
libraries of music and musical literature, with a chapter on private music collecting.

SAYERS, W. C. BERWICK. *Library Local Collections*. (Allen
& Unwin) 1939. All aspects of the formation of a 'local'
collection, i.e. a library of material on the topography,
history, antiquities, literary associations, industries,
trades, etc., of any particular locality; *A Manual of
Children's Libraries*. (Allen & Unwin) 1932. All aspects
of library work with young people, containing sections
on children's reading and the selection and care of books.

SPRATT, H. P. *Libraries for Scientific Research in Europe and America.* (Grafton) 1936. Short accounts of many research libraries personally visited by the author.

WILSON, L. R., and TAUBER, M. F. *The University Library: Its Organisation, Administration and Functions.* (University of Chicago Press, Chicago; Cambridge University Press, London) 1945.

LIBRARY CO-OPERATION

NEWCOMBE, LUXMOORE. *Library Co-operation in the British Isles.* (Allen & Unwin) 1937. The story of the development of library co-operation, describing the National Central Library and the whole system of inter-lending in Great Britain.

PAFFORD, J. H. P. *Library Co-operation in Europe.* (Library Association) 1935. The theory and practice of library co-operation and a description of its organization in 16 countries.

RIDER, FREMONT. *The Scholar and the Future of the Research Library: A Problem and its Solution.* (Hadham Press, New York) 1944. The problem is the tremendous growth of research libraries. The author's solution is the reproduction of research volumes on micro-cards and the co-operative publication of such micro-cards.

[*The dates quoted after titles are as far as possible those of the latest revised editions.*]

INDEX

Printed in the United States
By Bookmasters